A HANDBOOK ON ANTI-MAU MAU OPERATIONS

FOREWORD

This handbook has been prepared to assist the training and operations of troops in Kenya. Much assistance has been obtained from the Malaya publication "The Conduct of Anti-Terrorist Operations in Malaya" but the problem in Kenya is different in many respects.

This is much more a book of ideas than a book of rules.

The operations in Kenya place much responsibility on junior leaders and even individual soldiers. A very high standard of fieldcraft and marksmanship is required. All ranks must be physically fit and be imbued with a spirit of determination to close with the enemy.

We certainly must not overrate our enemy. He is a rotten shot, poorly armed and he seldom stays to fight. But he is a master at fieldcraft and concealment. This handbook is intended to help you to get to grips with him.

George Erskine.

General,
Commander-in-Chief,
EAST AFRICA.

A HANDBOOK ON ANTI-MAU MAU OPERATIONS

CONTENTS

Foreword

PAGE

Chapter I
INTRODUCTION

SECTION 1	General	1
SECTION 2	Geography and Climate	1
SECTION 3	Game	2

Chapter II
MAU MAU ORGANISATION

SECTION 1	General	3
SECTION 2	Mau Mau Aims	3
SECTION 3	Organisation	3
SECTION 4	Strengths	4
SECTION 5	Further Information	5

Chapter III
COMMAND AND CONTROL OF SECURITY FORCES

SECTION 1	General	6
SECTION 2	Emergency Committees	6

Chapter IV
INTELLIGENCE ORGANISATION

SECTION 1	General	8
SECTION 2	Special Branch Organisation and Tasks	8
SECTION 3	Information provided by Special Branch	9
SECTION 4	Intelligence responsibilities of the Services	9

Chapter V
OPERATIONS IN KENYA

SECTION 1	General	11
SECTION 2	Types of Operation	12
SECTION 3	Categories of Operational Areas	13
SECTION 4	The need for Trackers and War Dogs	14

Chapter VI
TRACKING THE MAU MAU

SECTION 1	Introduction to Visual Tracking	15
SECTION 2	The Handling of Trackers	15
SECTION 3	Trails and Tracks	17
SECTION 4	Mau Mau Signs and Fieldcraft	21
SECTION 5	Conclusion	24

Chapter VII
USE OF WAR DOGS

SECTION 1	General	25
SECTION 2	Training	25
SECTION 3	The Tracker Dog	26
SECTION 4	The Infantry Patrol Dog	29
SECTION 5	Dog Handlers	32
SECTION 6	Conclusion	33

Chapter VIII
PATROLLING—GENERAL

SECTION 1	Introduction	34
SECTION 2	Leadership and Morale	34
SECTION 3	Briefing and De-briefing	35
SECTION 4	Patrol Areas	36
SECTION 5	Size and Composition of Patrols	37
SECTION 6	Silent Signals	37
SECTION 7	Big Game	38
APPENDIX "A"	Patrol Order Aide-Memoire	39
APPENDIX "B"	De-briefing *Pro forma*	42
APPENDIX "C"	Bulldozer Procedure	44

Chapter IX
PATROLLING—TACTICS

SECTION 1	Patrol Formations	46
SECTION 2	Fieldcraft and Movement	47
SECTION 3	Patrol Bases	49
SECTION 4	Return to Base Drill	52
SECTION 5	Conclusion	53

Chapter X
AMBUSHES

SECTION 1	General	54
SECTION 2	Forest Ambushes	54
SECTION 3	Road Ambushes	55

Chapter XI
DRILL FOR ATTACKING A HIDE ON INFORMATION

SECTION 1	General	56
SECTION 2	Sequence of Action..	58
SECTION 3	The Assault..	60
SECTION 4	The Follow-up	60
SECTION 5	The Support Group	61
SECTION 6	Stops	62
SECTION 7	Summary	62
APPENDIX "A"	Suggested Composition of Assault Group and Weapons Carried	63
APPENDIX "B"	Diagram	65

Chapter XII
SWEEPS

SECTION 1	Introduction..	66
SECTION 2	Organisation	66
SECTION 3	Stop Parties	66
SECTION 4	Sweep Parties	67
SECTION 5	Reserves	69
SECTION 6	General	70
SECTION 7	Sweeps in the Forest	72

Chapter XIII
IMMEDIATE ACTION DRILLS

SECTION 1	Introduction..	73
SECTION 2	IA Drills required	73
SECTION 3	Encircling Attack	73
SECTION 4	Immediate Ambush	74
SECTION 5	Immediate Assault..	76
SECTION 6	Immediate Assault on Terrorist Camps..	76

Chapter XIV
AIR OPERATIONS

SECTION 1	General	78
SECTION 2	Types of Support	79
SECTION 3	Methods of Calling for Air Support	83
APPENDIX "A"	Aide-Memoire for demanding Air Support	83
APPENDIX "B"	Diagram	85

Chapter XV
TRAINING

Section 1	General	86
Section 2	Training before arrival in East Africa	86
Section 3	Initial Training in East Africa	88
Section 4	Training to maintain Operational Efficiency	89
Appendix "A"	List of Swahili Words	90
Appendix "B"	Notes on Construction of a Jungle Range	95

Chapter XVI
FIELD ENGINEERING

Section 1	Introduction	98
Section 2	Fieldworks	98
Section 3	Clearing Trees and Bamboo	99
Section 4	Use of Explosives	99
Section 5	Mine Detectors	101
Section 6	Booby Traps	102
Section 7	Roads and Tracks	102
Section 8	Field Accommodation	103
Diagram A	Layout of Tent	105
Diagram B	Details of Tent Construction	106
Diagram C	Method of Raising Flysheet	107
Diagram D	Desert Rose Urinal	108
Diagram E	Shallow Trench Urinal	109
Diagram F	Improvised Grease Trap	110
Diagram G	Improvised Oil Drum Incinerator	110

Chapter XVII
SIGNAL COMMUNICATIONS

Section 1	General	111
Section 2	Types of Wireless Sets	111
Section 3	Wireless Nets	112
Section 4	Overcoming Local Difficulties	113
Section 5	Aerials	114
Section 6	Conclusion	116
Appendix "A"	The Construction of the Shirley Aerial	116
Appendix "B"	Half-wave Folded Dipole Construction	122
Appendix "C"	Improved Aerials for the WS 31 and WS 88	123

Chapter XVIII
THE USE OF ANIMAL TRANSPORT

SECTION 1	General	136
SECTION 2	Uses and Limitations	136
SECTION 3	Responsibilities	137
SECTION 4	Employment	137
SECTION 5	The Fitting of Pack Saddles	138
SECTION 6	Roping and Loading	138
SECTION 7	Loads	140
SECTION 8	March Discipline	141
SECTION 9	Care of Animals	143
SECTION 10	Carriage of Animals by Road	145
SECTION 11	Care of Sick and Injured	146
SECTION 12	Conclusion	147

Chapter XIX
OPERATIONAL SUPPLY

SECTION 1	Operational Rations	148
SECTION 2	P.O.L.	149
SECTION 3	Means of Delivery	150
SECTION 4	Air Supply	150
APPENDIX "A"	Types of Rations—General	151
APPENDIX "B"	British—Compo	152
APPENDIX "C"	British—24-hour	154
APPENDIX "D"	African—Scale 9	155
APPENDIX "E"	Ancillaries: Self-heating beverages, Hexamine cookers, Rum/Tea	156

Chapter XX
FIRST AID AND PREVENTATIVE MEDICINES

SECTION 1	First Aid	157
SECTION 2	First Aid to Health	163
SECTION 3	Evacuation of Casualties	166

CHAPTER I
INTRODUCTION
Section 1—General

1. This handbook is not intended to be an all embracing tactical guide but to apply solely to the peculiar conditions which obtain in Kenya at the time of publication. The information and advice contained in it has been obtained from practical experience of these conditions. Finally, the longer chapters need, in most instances, only be read by those specialists on whose duties the subject matter has a bearing.

Section 2—Geography and Climate

2. The climate in Kenya is mainly temperate. There are heavy rains in March and April and again in October and November. These rains are often sufficiently heavy to put second class roads completely out of action and to necessitate restriction on the use of main roads. From May to September the weather is generally overcast with intermittent periods of clear skies. From December to February there are few clouds. Apart from the variations of temperature produced by cloud or sunshine, temperatures vary to a very great extent according to the altitude. The Nairobi area is between 5,000 and 6,000 feet, the native reserves in the operational areas are mostly between 6,000 and 7,000 feet, whilst the operational areas of the forests and mountain moorland may be anything between 8,000 and 12,000 feet, heights which impose considerable strain on troops compelled to operate in them.

3. The lower slopes of both Mt Kenya and the Aberdares are thickly forested, the higher parts of the forest being mainly bamboo which gives way to high altitude moorland on the upper slopes. Both the normal forest and the bamboo present a considerable obstacle to movement.

4. At the middle altitudes the temperature is about 40° at night and rises to a maximum of 90° in the day at the hotter times of the year. During the cloudy periods, temperatures are cool even in the daytime. Above the 9,000 ft. contours there are night frosts, and the top of Mount Kenya is snow-capped and shares with Mount Kilimanjaro the distinction of possessing one of the two glaciers in Africa.

Section 3—Game

5. There is a wide variety of game in East Africa. The game which has a significance on current operations is the big game which abounds plentifully in the Mount Kenya and Aberdare forests. The many thousands of elephants, rhinoceros and buffalo which live in these forests can be both an asset and a hindrance. The game tracks which they make have honeycombed the forests and in many cases are usable by pack transport; conversely their presence at night has sprung ambushes and when in large herds has caused confusion resulting in some instances in complete patrols being obliged to take to the trees.

CHAPTER II

MAU MAU ORGANIZATION

Section 1—General

1. **The Aim** of this chapter is to describe in general terms terrorist fighting and administrative organization.

2. It is inevitable that the description should be a generalization. It describes the organization that Mau Mau has been attempting to develop. Generally the organization is less developed than this chapter suggests, because its growth has never become complete due to security force action and other reasons.

3. **The Militant Wing** is the fighting element of the Mau Mau.

4. **The Passive Wing** is that part of Mau Mau which supplies the necessary administrative support to the militant wing.

5. **Komerera** are deserters from Mau Mau, and at the same time fugitives from justice.

Section 2—Mau Mau Aims

6. **The Strategical Aim** is to expand the security threat to an extent which will be beyond the capacity of Government to contain. The strategical aim has the ultimate objective of forcing Government to meet Kikuyu political demands.

7. **The Tactical Aim** of Mau Mau is to expand its military forces and deploy them to the extent necessary to achieve the strategical aim.

Section 3—Organization

8. **Group Organization.**—Mau Mau is organized in three main groups based on Nairobi and its immediate surroundings, the Aberdares and Mount Kenya. Each group is controlled by a committee, the members of which are the Chairmen of subordinate passive and militant committees.

9. **District Organizations.**—Each group contains a number of districts. Each district has a committee, the members of which are again drawn on from the Chairmen of subordinate passive and militant committees.

10. **Locational Organizations.**—The Mau Mau ideal is to have one major gang for each location. The administrative needs of this gang, in terms of food, money and other supplies are provided by the passive organization within the location.

11. **Control.**—The above organization suggests a high degree of control. In fact this does not exist and is prevented by communication difficulties and personal differences between leaders. Effective control only exists at locational level.

12. **Gangs.**—Major locational gangs are based on the forest except in the case of the Nairobi groups. A proportion of each gang is normally operating within the reserves or in the settled areas, the proportion varying considerably from time to time, depending upon a number of factors including seasonal ones such as the harvest.

Section 4—Strengths

13. **Personnel.**—The maximum number of terrorists within armed gangs based on the Aberdare and Mount Kenya Forests has been maintained at a strength of approximately 7,000. This Army or Militant Wing is supported by the non-militant wing within the normal reserve population, and receives from it recruits to replace losses. Only recently has the rate of replacements been smaller than the rate of kills and surrenders.

14. **Arms.**—The terrorists have about 1,000 precision firearms, and in addition a large and unknown number of home-made weapons. The latter are not effective in combat, but are effective in intimidating the population.

15. **Ammunition.**—One of the major factors restricting the scale of terrorist operations is the availability of ammunition particularly .303. Its security is therefore of permanent importance.

Section 5—Further Information

16. Mau Mau organization is subject to change and new facts are constantly being brought to light through the activities of the Military and Police Intelligence organizations. Information giving the current situation in detail is contained in:

(a) *Provincial and District Intelligence Summaries* which are issued at fortnightly and weekly intervals respectively.

(b) *The Kenya Intelligence Survey* issued by General Headquarters at approximately fortnightly intervals.

(c) *Research Papers* issued periodically by General Headquarters.

CHAPTER III

COMMAND AND CONTROL OF SECURITY FORCES

Section 1—General

1. The activities of Government and Security Forces to end the State of Emergency are co-ordinated at Colony, Province, District and Divisional level by the War Council and the Provincial, District and Divisional Emergency Committees.

2. The War Council consists of the Governor, Commander-in-Chief, the Deputy Governor and the European Minister without Portfolio. Ministers of Government are invited to attend when matters affecting their Portfolio are being considered. It meets twice weekly and specially as required. It is served by a Secretariat which includes military officers and which forms part of the Cabinet Office.

3. Action on decisions made by the War Council is taken as a rule by the various Ministers of Government and by General Headquarters, East Africa. There are occasions, however, when action is made the responsibility of the Provincial Emergency Committees who, in any case, are kept informed of the decisions of the War Council.

4. The Commander-in-Chief exercises overall command of the three fighting services and operational command over the Police and the Kikuyu Guard.

Section 2—Emergency Committees

5. The Provincial Emergency Committees consist of the Provincial Commissioner, as Chairman, a senior military representative (usually the Commander of the Brigade conducting operations in the Province—if two Brigades are operating, both Brigade Commanders attend or are represented), the officer in charge of the Police in the Province (usually an Assistant Commissioner of Police) and a representative of the unofficial interests, usually a Member of Legislative Council. In addition the Deputy Director of Operations often attends meetings of the Provincial Emergency Committees.

6. These Committees meet once weekly and specially as required. They are served by an Executive Officer. The Committees have a direct channel of approach to the War Council. The Provincial Emergency Committees are responsible for co-ordinating Government, Army and Police activities to end the Emergency in their Provinces, within the policy prescribed by the War Council or by the Commander-in-Chief. The Provincial Emergency Committees (PEC's) in the affected area are:—

    The Central Province Emergency Committee.

    The Rift Valley Province Emergency Committee.

    The Southern Province Emergency Committee.

    The Nairobi Extra-Provincial District Emergency Committee (which has the status of a P.E.C.).

7. Below the Provincial Emergency Committees there are Emergency Committees for each District in the affected area and for most Divisions within Districts. Their composition is as follows:—

District Emergency Committee	*Divisional Emergency Committee*
District Commissioner	District Officer.
Senior Army Officer in the District.	Senior Army Officer in the Division.
Senior Police Officer in the District.	Senior Police Officer in the Division.
Unofficial representative (only in the settled areas).	

    Nearly all District Emergency Committees are served by District Executive Officers.

CHAPTER IV

INTELLIGENCE ORGANIZATION

Section 1—General

1. **The Aim** of this chapter is to describe in general terms the intelligence organization in Kenya.

2. The chapter should be read bearing in mind that it describes the organization that is being aimed at, and which is still in process of development.

3. **Operational Intelligence Requirement.**—The requirement is to provide:—

   (a) The operational commanders with that general planning information concerning terrorist locations, strengths, intentions, etc., which will enable them to dispose their forces to the best advantage.

   (b) Troops on the ground with that information which will enable them to make contacts.

4. **Responsibility.**—With the exception of that in Section 4 below, the responsibility for meeting the operational intelligence requirement rests with the Police Special Branch.

Section 2—Special Branch Organizaton and Tasks

5. **Special Branch** is deployed at Colonial, Provincial and District level. Its permanent establishment is designed to meet the peace-time requirement for political and security intelligence and is not designed to meet the emergency requirements at paragraph 3 above.

6. **An Emergency Increment** has been supplied accordingly to Special Branch to enable it to meet the additional operational intelligence requirement. This increment provides at district level a District Military Intelligence Officer (U.K. based) and a number of Field Intelligence Officers (locally based) varying in number from four to six per district. At Provincial level there is a Provincial Military Intelligence Officer and an interrogation element. The increments are largest in the reserves and smallest in the settled areas.

7. **The Military Intelligence Officer's Task** is to:—

(a) Provide Commanders with the necessary planning information.

(b) Control, in conjunction with his Special Branch Officer, Field Intelligence Officers.

8. **The Field Intelligence Officer's Task** is to obtain contact information from covert sources.

Section 3—Information Provided by Special Branch

9. **Immediate Information** is passed automatically and immediately to the nearest unit or formation.

10. **Planning Information** is provided at periodical briefings.

11. **Limitations.**—Planning information is adequate. The provision of contact information is not yet satisfactory, and its expansion depends largely on the amount of supervision that Military Intelligence Officers can give to Field Intelligence Officers and it is particularly important that they should avoid using them as formation and unit Intelligence Officers. It is also desirable that Commanders should not ask for too frequent briefings.

Section 4—Intelligence Responsibilities of the Services

12. **G.H.Q.** has the special responsibilities for:—

(a) Handling photographic interpretation.

(b) Conducting long-term research into Mau Mau Passive and Militant organizations.

13. **Formation and Unit Intelligence Officers.**—These officers are available to formations and units for employment in the usual ways. They should be used particularly for:—

(a) Liaison with Special Branch.

(b) Ensuring that information obtained by units reaches Special Branch.

14. **Interrogation.**—Immediate interrogation is carried out at unit, etc. level, at the place and time of capture. The interrogation should be rapid and confined to establishing terrorist locations. Prisoners should not be retained by units for longer than 24 hours, unless they are required as guides for immediate ground operations, in which case the permission of the formation commander must be obtained.

Deliberate interrogation is carried out by Special Branch.

15. **Air Photography.**—The photographic interpretation resources are primarily used to deal with the R.A.F. requirement for information. It is seldom, therefore, that unit demands for the photographing and interpretation of an area can be met. Positive interpretation results produced for the R.A.F. are, however, in all cases passed to the formation concerned, and provide much useful information, particularly in the case of targets which for one reason or another are not attacked from the air. In addition, photographic mosaics of the Aberdares and Mount Kenya forest areas are available.

CHAPTER V

OPERATIONS IN KENYA

Section 1—General

1. The tactics which have been evolved in Kenya have been designed to meet the particular terrain in which operations take place and to overcome an enemy whose characteristics are different from those of any other enemy against which British Forces have been deployed for many years.

2. The Mau Mau are fleet of foot, silent in movement, highly experienced in fieldcraft and normally anxious to avoid action with all forms of organized Military Forces. The qualities which must be developed in troops engaged against the Mau Mau are therefore those required to track down and shoot shy game.

3. Soldiers must accordingly learn to be experts at the quick snapshot at a moving target, to move quickly and silently in the jungle, to read the few tell tale signs of Mau Mau activity in the jungle, which the cunning of the enemy has now reduced to a minimum and to acquire a high degree of stamina and physical fitness.

4. **Tracker/Combat Teams.**—In order to meet the special operational conditions, every major unit engaged in anti-Mau Mau operations has formed at least one tracker/combat team composed of six picked men, augmented by two African trackers, a tracker dog and handler, a patrol dog and handler. Tracker/combat teams are commanded by an officer who has received special training in tracking, use of trackers and war dogs and in advanced Mau Mau fieldcraft. These teams are used for any special tasks requiring a high degree of fieldcraft and endurance. The composition of tracker/combat teams differs little from the standard "all purpose" patrol recommended in Chapter VIII. It should be the aim of all unit commanders progressively to raise the standard of all their rank and file until that of their tracker/combat team is reached by all patrols.

The Kenya Police

5. Military operations are frequently carried out in conjunction with the Kenya Police, who are widely deployed in the

troubled areas and whose organization includes mobile General Service Units (G.S.Us.), which approximate to the strength of an Infantry platoon.

6. **Police Tracker Teams.**—In areas where cattle thefts are most prevalent, Police tracker teams have been formed with the dual role of recovering stolen stock and destroying the gangs responsible for the thefts.

The Kikuyu Guard

7. The Kikuyu Guard is an organization of armed loyalists commanded by European District Officers. It provides centres of armed resistance in the Reserves, guides for the Army and Police on specific operations and additional manpower for sweeps and cordoning operations.

Section 2—Types of Operation

8. There are four main types of operation in Kenya:—

(a) *Assistance to Police and Civil Administration in the Main Towns, i.e. Nairobi, Nakuru, Nanyuki, etc.*

In these operations the military carry out the cordoning of the area, whilst the police search the area. The planning of the operations is carried out by a joint staff of Military, Police and Civil Administration. Whilst the whole operation may last several days it is usual for each particular operation to last about eight hours.

The Military role is very simple and may involve:—

(i) Cordoning.

(ii) Guarding detainee cages.

(iii) Escorting detained persons to cages.

(b) *Assistance to the Police and Civil Administration in the Prevention of Stock Thefts, etc., in the European Farming Areas.*

In this role Military forces are normally widely dispersed. The cattle bomas (enclosures) are usually raided at night and Military, Police and special tracker teams take over pursuit of gangs and cattle at dawn. Operations are in two forms:—

(i) *Prevention of Thefts, etc.*—Done by patrols around farms, etc., either by armoured cars, or by infantry mounted in vehicles or on foot.

(ii) *Pursuit of Gangs after Incidents.*—This is done by formation or unit tracker teams. The essence is speed, to catch up with the gangs before they have entered the forest. Commanders of pursuing patrols or tracker teams receive special training in handling native trackers at the Command Battle School. The rank and file must be capable of a high degree of mobility in order to gain on the marauders and be sufficiently good marksmen to engage successfully, fleeting targets. Special requirements for operating in the forests are shown below.

(c) *The Elimination of Terrorist Gangs in the Native Reserves and the Assistance to the Police and Civil Administration in the Restoration of Law and Order.*

A certain number of troops are deployed in bases in the Native Reserves. From these bases constant patrols, sweeps and cordon operations are carried out in conjunction with the Police and Kikuyu Guard. They are usually based on information received from captured terrorists or loyal African civilians. A further task is the assistance in training the Kikuyu Guard in small arms and minor tactics. Since the ground in the Reserves is extremely undulating, a high degree of fitness is required. Unit signallers must acquire the art of making the best use of ground for maintaining wireless contact.

(d) *The Complete Destruction of All Terrorists in the Prohibited Areas, i.e. Aberdare and Mount Kenya Forests, etc.*

These are purely Military operations and include the denial of food to terrorist gangs living in the prohibited areas. These operations are often carried out in conjunction with the R.A.F.

Section 3—Categories of Operational Areas

9. There are three specially defined types of Operational Areas in which the rules vary for the opening of fire by Security Forces.

(a) *Prohibited Areas*

Most of the forest and certain other areas have been declared prohibited. A member of the Security Forces is authorized to shoot on sight any person found in, or seen entering, a prohibited area.

(*b*) *Special Areas*

Virtually the entire area of operations in Kenya has been declared a Special Area. A member of the Security Forces may use lethal weapons in order to stop and submit to search any person who fails to stop when challenged in a Special Area.

(*c*) *Protected Areas*

Since a number of detention camps are outside the Special Areas, a small strip of land round each camp has been declared a Protected Area. Rules regarding the opening of fire by Security Forces in Protected Areas are the same as for Special Areas.

Section 4—The Need for Trackers and War Dogs

10. It will be appreciated from the foregoing that whether a patrol is following up a cattle theft in the settled areas, patrolling in the reserves or engaged on forest operations, the assistance of native trackers and war dogs is a great asset to it.

11. Trackers and war dogs are accordingly allocated to units engaged on anti-Mau Mau operations on a generous scale, and their use takes a high place in both the planning and execution of most operations.

12. Chapters in which the correct uses of native trackers and war dogs are described, therefore, precede those which give more detailed notes on Tactics in this handbook.

CHAPTER VI

TRACKING THE MAU MAU

Section 1—Introduction to Visual Tracking

1. The Mau Mau will rarely stand and fight; they make raids and return to their forest hideouts as quickly as possible. To make contact with them is difficult. One of the methods used to hunt down and kill the Mau Mau is by tracking. Tracking is used by Africans normally when hunting animals or finding strayed stock. Animals do not conceal their tracks and have set characteristics which, when known to the tracker, make animal hunting comparatively easy.

2. Tracking Mau Mau is very much more difficult. Realising that the Security Forces are using African trackers to hunt them down, the Mau Mau gangs are using all sorts of methods to conceal their tracks. Following the comparatively ill-defined human footprints, as compared with the well-defined hoof-marks made by game, is difficult enough without the Mau Mau concealing their tracks. Therefore first-class trackers must be used. Many Africans can track, but the first-class tracker is not found in the average African. He is born, and no amount of practice and experience will make the average tracker as good as the born tracker.

3. The method of making contact with gangs by tracking is nevertheless very successful and every effort must be made to keep up the morale of the trackers and realize their importance in patrols. They are part of the team.

Section 2—The Handling of Trackers

General

4. The African is simple, not very intelligent, but very willing if treated in the right way. Do not regard him as a slave or as an equal. You will find that most Africans have an innate respect for the White Man. This respect is easily increased or destroyed, depending on the treatment given to them.

5. The respect will be destroyed if familiarity is shown or they are allowed to take liberties. This does not mean that they should not be spoken to or offered cigarettes. They appreciate

cheerfulness and the odd joke. They have a good sense of humour which, although not entirely similar to that of the White Man, is none the less present. They dislike being sworn at, even in fun, and cannot understand sarcasm.

6. Small things, such as making them stand up when spoken to, are important. They should come under the direct control of the patrol commander and other members of the patrol should understand this.

The African Mentality

7. It must be understood that the African has a completely different view of life and code of morals from ours. He does not think of the future, which the White Man has difficulty in understanding and finds irritating.

Morale

8. A high standard of morale among trackers must be maintained, and this will depend mainly on how the Europeans in the patrol behave. They like to air their troubles, and these must be listened to.

Administration

9. Although their physical needs are a great deal less than ours, do not disregard the African's comfort. There is a scale of clothing and rations for African trackers, and it must be ensured that they get it.

Tracking Patrols

10. **Use of Correct Trackers.**—Not all trackers are of the same tribe. The normally forest dwelling trackers, such as the Kikuyu-Derobo, Mau Derobo, Kipsigis-Lumbwa Nderobo, will be more satisfactory in the forest than the trackers who come from the low country, such as the Samburu, Masai, Kamba and Turkhana, who are more useful in tracking across the dry grass country. Care should therefore be taken that the trackers in operational use by battalions are from the tribes most suited to the terrain in which the battalion is located.

11. **Composition of Tracking Group in a Patrol.**—The ideal is a group of three trackers and one scout or bodyguard. Owing to the shortage of first-class trackers within the Command, more often only two trackers and one scout are used.

12. **Formation Using Three Trackers.**—A tracker leads the patrol on the tracks which he is following. Behind the leading tracker is his bodyguard or scout. Following the bodyguard are the other two trackers, one watching for tracks breaking off to the right and the other watching left. This formation is only used when the patrol is canalized in the forest, and is adapted to suit open country according to circumstances.

13. **Formation Using Two Trackers.**—The formation is identical, except that only one tracker follows the bodyguard and has to watch for tracks breaking right and left.

14. **The Bodyguard.**—The duty of the bodyguard is exactly the same as that of a leading scout in a normal patrol. The trackers all have their eyes to the ground and therefore cannot look out for ambushes, camps, or the enemy.

15. **The Duty of the Trackers.**—The duty of the trackers is to track. They should not be made to carry heavy loads or become odd-job men. They should be trained in the use of firearms, silent signals, IA drills, and to pass all information to their patrol commander.

Action on Finding Tracks

16. Upon encountering tracks it is essential that some small time be spent in studying them, as invaluable information can be obtained, such as when the gang passed the spot, the numbers, whether they were laden (i.e. food carriers or armed members), and direction. It is also important that the spot is fixed on the map.

Summary

17. In tracking down Mau Mau, persistence, alertness, silence, and the ability to shoot straight and quickly, are important. Be firm yet fair, and study your trackers for their individual peculiarities.

Section 3—Trails and Tracks

Introduction

18. To move silently and quickly in most parts of the forests is impossible unless use is made of trails. There are a considerable number of paths in the forest, originally made by big game

during their nightly or seasonal migrations. Since big game animals find difficulty in climbing or descending steep, slippery slopes, it will be found that game trails are very easy going, the inclines being gentle.

19. Both the Mau Mau and our own patrols use these trails when quick, silent movement is required. Always check for Mau Mau tracks when using these trails and remember that it is on these trails that ambushes are easily laid, both by security forces and the Mau Mau, though the latter, to date, have not taken full advantage of the opportunity offered.

20. Tracks on trails are inclined to be quickly obliterated by game and rain, as some trails are so wide that there is little overhead cover.

Types of Trails

21. **Ridge Crest Trails.**—Formed by game along main ridges to enable movement from one part of the country to another. Usually well defined and useful for rapid movement in thick forest, but not used to a great extent by Mau Mau for fear of leaving tracks on trails used frequently by security forces.

22. **Contour Trails.**—Found only in area of shallow valleys and generally join crests of ridges by following the contours round the head of the valley. Used by Mau Mau considerably, to enable them to have easy routes to their camps.

23. **Spur Trails.**—These follow the small spurs often found projecting from main ridges into deep valleys. Often rather vague, but are useful for crossing heavy country across the grain. Again used considerably by Mau Mau.

Common Tracks

24. **Man.**—Barefoot prints are soft rounded impressions formed by the heel, ball of foot, or toes. Women's tracks are generally smaller and have on the whole two characteristics. Firstly, they tend to be pigeon-toed, and secondly, their toes are more splayed out than the males.

25. **Animals.**—Due to the fact that most animals have cloven hooves, the impressions formed on the ground have sharp, clear-cut edges.

Tracking

26. The following are signs the experienced tracker looks for when tracking spoor:—
    - (a) Crushed and bent grass and vegetation.
    - (b) Broken twigs and leaves.
    - (c) Overturned leaves.
    - (d) Mud displaced from streams.
    - (e) Cobwebs.
    - (f) The state of the dew on a trail.
    - (g) Mud or scratches on stones and logs.
    - (h) Moss scraped from trees.

27. **Running Men.**—Points to observe are skid marks, depth of impression, running on balls of feet and toes, splayed out toes and badly damaged vegetation with resultant lack of concealment of trail.

28. **Loaded Men.**—Short footsteps, deeper impressions than normal in soft ground, and toes splayed out.

29. **Judging the Age of Tracks.**—
    - (a) *Weather*: The state of the weather—rain, wind, sunshine—should always be recorded in one's mind as it is one of the most important points in deciding the age of a track.
    - (b) *Vegetation*: The state and position of trodden vegetation; various grasses have different grades of resilience and only practice and experience can enable a tracker to use this factor for accurate ageing of a track.
    - (c) *Impressions in mud*: Always note the state of dryness of a track in mud or soft ground. If the track is very fresh, water will not have run back into the depression made by a foot. Later the water runs back, and later still the mud which has been pushed up round the depression and the mud kicked forward by the foot leaving the ground, begins to dry.
    - (d) *Obliteration by rain, or dripping from mist*: By remembering when it last rained, more accurate judgment of the age of tracks is easy. If the tracks are pock-marked, obviously they were made before the rain, and if they

are not pock-marked they were made after the rain. Similarly, by looking to see if the tracks have been pock-marked by mist dripping from trees, the age can be better judged.

(e) *Cracks in bent grass or leaves*: An indication of the age of a track may be gained by the state of dryness of these cracks. When fresh they are green, but after a few days turn a brown colour. Again the amount of sunshine and rain during the last few days should be taken into account.

(f) *Game tracks superimposed*: Remember that most animals lie up during the day and move about at night. Therefore if human prints on main forest tracks have animal tracks superimposed, and these tracks show that the game have moved in both directions, the human prints are probably at least one night old. If the animal tracks show that game have moved only in one direction, then the human tracks were probably made during the night, after the game had moved down to salt or water but before the game moved back.

(g) *Leaves covering tracks*: In the forest leaves are always falling from the trees. The number of leaves that fall depends on wind and rain. By looking at the number of leaves covering the tracks and taking into consideration the amount of wind and rain during the past few days, another indication as to the age of tracks is obtained. Remember that in Kenya we have no Autumn and that leaves fall from trees all the year round.

Conclusion

30. A tracker has many things to consider whilst tracking. He must possess certain qualities, such as extraordinary eyesight, memory, intelligence, fitness, and understanding of Nature. Although practice and experience will make the average man a tracker, he can never be as good as the born tracker, for the real tracker is born, not made. African trackers track best in the areas in which they were born, and when moved to new areas must be given time to become used to the climatic conditions and the difference in vegetation and soils. Patience, persistence and acute observation are the basis of good tracking.

Section 4—Mau Mau Signs and Fieldcraft

Introduction

31. The Mau Mau have their own methods of informing members of their gangs where they have gone, or where they have hidden their food, and they also have their own warning system. These can be spotted by an alert patrol. The examples of signs given below are old and were only effective in certain areas. Signs vary from area to area and from gang to gang. Patrols should attempt to recognize new signs and pass back all information regarding these signs. The interrogation of prisoners must include the finding out of signs. The examples were noted up to the end of April, 1953, and are only given as a guide as to what to expect. All signs are as inconspicuous as possible in order to conceal them from the security forces.

32. **Direction Signs.**—Direction signs as below are usually found at track junctions:—

   (a) *Bent bamboo.*—Bent down and pointing in the direction required. Inconspicuous as it is usually interpreted as having been done by big game.

   (b) *Bamboo leaves crossed* and pinned to the ground with a twig, the longest arm of the cross indicating direction.

   (c) *Bamboo bent across a path* indicates either ambush or warning to Mau Mau that the path is known to security forces.

   (d) *The food cache sign.*—Three small holes are dug at regular distances up the middle of the path. At right angles to one of these, a hole is dug on either side of the path. These are lined up with a conspicuous tree or bamboo in which there is a panga cut. By placing a panga in the cut and sighting along the blade the direction to a food cache is obtained.

   (e) *Abandoned hide.*—A tree near the abandoned hide is indicated by cutting off a large piece of bark. The lowest branch of the tree points in the direction of the new hide. The branch merely indicates the direction. The new hide will not be visible, but by following the indicated line, tracks leading to the new hide will be found. The new hide may be a considerable distance away.

33. Concealment of Tracks.—

(a) Walking backwards, mainly in soft ground or dusty patches. Note that the mud flakes being kicked up are kicked up by the heel instead of the toe. The heel mark tends to be deeper than that of the ball of the foot and the feet are placed wider apart although the pace is shorter.

(b) Walking on the edges of or astride paths.

(c) Stepping in one another's tracks—used also to disguise numbers in a gang.

(d) Use of streams and stream beds.

(e) Splitting up into small groups or individuals over easy tracking ground or on nearing hideout.

(f) Bent bamboo: Should it be necessary for a gang to cross a wide path, the last member pulls down a bamboo or bush with ample foliage to cover the tracks. This also is frequently interpreted as having been done by big game.

(g) Walking along fallen trees, over rocky ground, or stepping from rock to rock.

(h) Stolen cattle:

    (i) Dragging bush over trail;

    (ii) Splitting herds and mixing with herds of other farms.

(j) Other tricks:

    (i) Tip-toeing;

    (ii) rear man covering tracks with bamboo leaves;

    (iii) False tracks;

    (iv) Gang walking in each others footprints, rear man cutting off the feet of dead elephant or rhino and tying them to his feet and obliterating human footprints.

34. Concealment of Hideouts.—

The main methods used are:—

(a) Concealment of tracks leading to hideout.

(b) Use of many devious entrance tracks.

(c) Sighting hideout in most unlikely places, usually close to a commanding position where the gang can lie up during the daylight hours.

35. Types of Hideout.—

(a) Underground—spoil thrown into the river and the entrance concealed. In forest these may be large and accommodate large numbers, but in Reserves are normally for only one or two men.

(b) Caves under waterfalls—all sizes used.

(c) Hut hideouts in Reserve—holes dug under beds capable of holding up to five men, having small concealed entrances.

(d) Trees—often two- or three-man hides in holes amongst the roots of large trees. The shells of burnt-out trees are sometimes used as sentry boxes or O.Ps.

(e) Lie-ups where no form of construction is erected, the gang merely lying up under naturally thick cover.

(f) Armed members of some gangs live separately from the food carriers. In many gangs the women members are segregated, and in some cases the gang leader lives close by them.

36. Keeping Up to Date.—Tracking humans who are always trying to conceal their tracks is difficult, even for an experienced African tracker, who is more used to tracking animals. Just as the method of breaking and entering used by a burglar will often give his identity away to the Police, so the methods by which a gang conceals its tracks, and the way it establishes its hideouts, will give away the gang. Therefore it is essential that all new methods of concealing tracks be brought to the notice of your tracker, and, conversely, if he finds new methods, the information should be passed back.

Section 5—Conclusion

37. When a patrol is sent out with trackers it is essential that the patrol commander himself has a fair knowledge of tracking. This knowledge may be more theoretical than practical but he should be able to recognize signs when pointed out to him by his trackers. As trackers will sometimes have different opinions as to what certain signs or tracks indicate, the patrol commander must have sufficient knowledge to make a final decision.

38. In British units language difficulties between patrol commander and trackers can be most tiresome. The good patrol commander will learn enough Kiswahili to eliminate this difficulty. Just as the trackers must be patient when tracking so must the patrol commander be patient when dealing with his trackers. The basis of successful tracking patrols is the team spirit which lies within all the members of the patrol.

CHAPTER VII

USE OF WAR DOGS

Section 1—General

1. Only two types of war dogs are used by Infantry battalions in Kenya:—
   (a) The Tracker Dog.
   (b) The Infantry Patrol Dog.

These are two completely different types of dog with quite different roles. The ways in which they work, their uses and limitations, and the correct way of employing them must be clearly understood.

2. War dogs properly used give us an advantage over the enemy and are a valuable weapon. The fullest use should therefore be made of them.

3. It must be realized that a dog is an animal and not a machine. This self-evident fact is often forgotten. No matter how well trained it is, its performance is never constant and from time to time, when having an "off" day, it will cause disappointment by its indifferent performance.

4. The efficiency of the dog is in direct ratio to that of the handler. It follows therefore that the selection of suitable men for training as dog handlers is all important.

5. Officers and N.C.O.s must not only be capable of getting the maximum use out of their dogs in the field, they must also be capable of supervising their management and training when not on operations.

Section 2—Training

6. All dogs are trained to a high standard before they are sent out to battalions. It is, however, up to the handler to put a final "polish" on the dog's performance by working him on operations or under operational conditions.

7. The training of the dog must go on continually and handlers must be allowed sufficient time to do this.

8. All dogs are trained on the "Reward for Work" system. Even when fully trained, all dogs are required to work successfully before they are fed.

9. Other principles of training are:—
   (a) Firmness and Kindness (not to be confused with softness).
   (b) Training periods must always end on a successful note. A dog should never be returned at once to kennels if he fails to work properly—to do so will encourage him to become an inveterate "lead swinger". He must be given a simple task and made to do it successfully before he is fed and returned to kennels.
   (c) Training periods should not be too long and should be as varied as possible. The quarry, type of country, time, weather conditions, etc., should be varied each day.

Section 3—The Tracker Dog

General

10. All tracker dogs in Kenya are handled by R.A.V.C. men who are attached for all purposes to battalions.

11. The dog is trained to follow human ground scent and it is immaterial whether the scent is that of an African, Asian or European. The dog will normally follow the freshest track, but he will, if "given the scent" from personal clothing or belongings, discriminate and follow the scent of that particular quarry.

12. The dog must be made "to sing for his supper", i.e. he must work successfully before being fed. This must occur even when fully trained. By using this method the interest of the dog in following a "track" is assured. Failure to find his quarry should automatically result in the dog being starved. On patrol when not required to work, the dog should be fed last thing in the evening after he has successfully followed a short track laid by a member of the patrol in the bivouac area. A similar procedure should be adopted when in camp or barracks. This procedure, involving as it does, extra work necessitates a high devotion to training principles on the part of the handler, and may, from time to time, require supervision.

It is important that the dog be fed or rewarded by some food as soon as possible after finding his quarry.

13. A high degree of physical fitness both in dog and handler is essential. In the case of the dog, long, slow exercise daily behind a jeep, bicycle, or horse will produce this. The handler must keep himself fit not only by the exercise he takes when exercising the dog, but also by sports, route marches, and cross-country running.

Scent

14. Every man gives off a scent which is peculiar to him alone. This scent is mingled with the smell of his clothing, equipment and footwear and with the scent given off by bruised vegetation, disturbed earth, crushed insects, etc., caused by the man's movement. This combination of scents produces a track "picture" which the dog follows. The concentration of the various component scents of this picture are continually changing, first one predominating and then another. It is when the track picture consists mainly of the scent of vegetation, earth, etc., that there is a risk of the dog "changing" on to a fresh quarry should a track of similar predominating scents cross that of the original.

15. Scenting conditions vary widely from place to place and minute to minute—indeed the immortal John Jorrocks said, "There's nothing so queer as scent 'cept women".

Thus, after tracking well for a time a dog may suddenly be at fault due to sudden deterioration of scent and, conversely, after a slow start scent may so improve that the track ends successfully.

16. Apart from obvious factors which cause the quarry to leave a strong scent, e.g. blood, dirty body and clothes, sweat, panic, etc., there are certain climatic factors which influence scenting conditions:—

Favourable

(*a*) Air and ground temperatures approximately the same.

(*b*) Dull, damp weather.

Adverse
- (a) Hot sun.
- (b) Strong winds.
- (c) Heavy rain.
- (d) Tarmac roads, rock and other hard surface.
- (e) Dust.
- (f) Running water.

17. From this can be deduced the following facts regarding scenting conditions in Kenya:—
- (a) The dogs will track well at night, in the early mornings, and late evenings.
- (b) The periods of the long and short rains will be favourable for tracking except when it is raining hard, and immediately afterwards.
- (c) The European Settled Areas will normally carry a good scent except during the heat of the day and in very dry weather.
- (d) The Native Reserves should carry a good scent, but the track picture will be confused due to the movement of large numbers of natives about the area.
- (e) The Forest should nearly always produce good conditions, but here the presence of game may cause confusion.
- (f) The employment of tracker dogs in towns and villages is very rarely worth while.

Under the most favourable conditions it will be quite feasible to follow tracks up to 12 hours "cold".

Under unfavourable conditions there may be no scent at all even if the quarry is only a few minutes ahead.

Operational Employment

18. TIME is all important. Therefore:—
- (a) The dog must be close up and readily available.
- (b) The decision to use the dog must be made at once and *not* as a last resort.

(c) Once the decision to use the dog is made, the area must not be "fouled". Therefore, all unnecessary movement in the area by troops, police, etc., must be rigidly controlled until the dog has got away on the scent.

(d) The tracker dog handler, who is armed only with a pistol, should be given an escort armed with an automatic weapon. The escort should be immediately behind the handler, with the rest of the patrol several yards behind.

(e) The degree of fatigue a dog has reached will determine its ability. Therefore, every effort should be made to produce the dog fresh, and not tired out by a long forced march.

(f) The handler should know from the dog's behaviour when he is nearing his quarry and will be able to tell the leader of the patrol.

(g) Fatigue on the part of the handler may spoil the dog's performance. The handler may unwittingly pull the dog off the scent, or discourage him from following the track through dense bush or awkward going. The patrol leader must be on his guard against this. It is also not unknown for the handler, due to fatigue, to say that there is no scent or that the dog is exhausted. A fit dog will aways be capable of going on longer than the handler.

Section 4—The Infantry Patrol Dog

General

19. The sole purpose of the Patrol dog is to give early warning to the patrol that there are other people in its vicinity.

20. This is does by using its exceptional powers of scent and/or hearing. It is worthy of notice that a dog's hearing ability is approximately ten times better than a human's, or to put it another way, they can hear at a mile what a human will hear at 175 yards.

21. The scent picked up by the dog is "air scent", i.e. scent carried down by air currents and wind from the man in hiding to the dog. It will be seen that air scent is quite different to the ground scent on which the tracker dog works.

22. The dog cannot discriminate between friend and foe, nor does it discriminate between European and African. It occasionally will "false point" at game, but this trait can be eradicated by the intelligent handler and further training.

23. The ability of a handler to "read" his dog is all important. This can only be achieved with time and experience. Handlers should, therefore, be changed as seldom as possible.

24. The distance at which warning is given depends on the following:—

(a) Wind direction and velocity.

(b) Concentration of scent and/or volume of sound.

(c) Scenting conditions.

(d) Density of vegetation.

(e) Individual inherent ability of dog and handler.

(f) Condition and fitness of dog.

In open grass country under good conditions, points at ranges up to 600 yards may be obtained, whereas in dense forest ranges may be reduced to only a few yards.

25. As with tracker dogs, training must be continuous and is based on the principle of "Reward only for Work".

26. The dog "points" by one or a combination of the following signs:—

(a) Raising the head and pricking the ears.

(b) Tensing of body.

(c) Tail wagging.

(d) Keenness to investigate.

It is immaterial how he does it providing there is no noise.

27. The success of a patrol dog depends on its ability to locate the enemy without itself being detected. In all cases a patrol dog will detect a hidden enemy before a human. He can be worked by day or night in most types of country.

Operational Employment

28. The dog can be worked:—

(a) On a lead.

(b) Loose in front of the patrol.

In both cases the dog must be under the control of his handler who will normally precede the patrol.

Both handler and dog have to be more highly trained if the dog is to work loose. Ability to do so should be the aim as the dog is much more effective if used this way.

To avoid unnecessary fatigue the dog should not be worked for unnecessarily long periods. Over insuring by using the dog in front of a patrol when there is little or no possibility of contact will reduce his efficiency.

29. The Patrol dog can be used:—

(a) On patrols.

(b) In sweeps.

(c) With stops.

(d) In ambush positions.

(e) As an outpost sentry.

Patrols

30. The handler should be warned for patrol as early as possible to obviate the possibility of the dog being fed just prior to being called out.

31. The dog and handler will normally lead the patrol. The handler will have to devote all his attention to working the dog. He will do this more efficiently, and will feel less conspicuous, if he is closely supported by an escort armed with an automatic weapon.

32. By night the patrol will be close up behind the handler. By day they can be further back providing they remain within easy visual signalling distance.

33. When the dog "points", the handler indicates by silent hand signal "Enemy in sight" and gives the direction.

Sweeps

34. Using one or more patrol dogs on sweeps will frequently speed up progress considerably. It will also ensure that thick cover is more effectively searched.

Stops, Ambushes and Sentries

35. In these roles the dog is static and is used to give timely warning of the enemy's approach.

The handler and dog are placed a short distance from the remainder of the group, the position being selected by the handler with due regard to the direction of the wind.

By day the distance should be within easy visual signal. At night, a simple signalling system can be devised, using a piece of string which can be jerked to alert everyone.

In ambush positions it is essential that the dog remains absolutely quiet and still. Any dog with a tendency to whine or growl when "pointing" should not be used.

Section 5—Dog Handlers

General

36. The performance of the war dog is directly dependent on the skill of the handler and the mutual understanding existing between him and his dog. The dog must only be handled by a trained handler.

The most highly trained dog in the hands of a poor handler will produce a very disappointing performance and it is regrettably only too easy for a good dog to be ruined in less than a week.

Selection of Handlers

37. The qualities required of a good handler are only found in the best type of soldier and it is consequently a waste of time and effort to select any but the best.

Men should possess the following qualities:—

(*a*) A sound basic military training.

(*b*) Volunteers.

(*c*) Friendly and sympathetic towards dogs.

(*d*) Intelligence.
(*e*) Patience and perseverance.
(*f*) Dependability.
(*g*) Resourcefulness.
(*h*) Physical fitness and stamina.

38. Previous experience with animals is desirable but not essential, but the type of men who invariably proves most suitable is one with a country background. The handling of tracker and patrol dogs is in many ways similar to the handling of foxhounds and the qualities required of a handler are similar to those found in a huntsman. Only a few men have the instinctive sympathy, knack and ability.

39. The advice of handlers should be sought when the use of dogs is being planned. Care is sometimes necessary in interpreting the advice given, as there is ocassionally a tendency for handlers to pose as "Oracles" and to try to turn themselves into a private army. This is easily controlled if an officer, who is really interested, is appointed in charge of all war dogs in the battalion. If this officer spends one or two days at the War Dog Wing of the East Africa Battle School he can acquire sufficient knowledge to enable him adequately to supervise the general management and training or employment of his battalion's dogs.

Section 6—Conclusion

40. Properly trained and used, war dogs are of great value to battalions engaged in the present anti-terrorist operations in Kenya. They bring to the troops whom they accompany keener senses than those enjoyed by human beings and in addition, that sixth sense which human beings usually acquire only after many years of fieldcraft.

41. It is, however, useless to expect much from war dogs if there is, within a battalion, general antipathy to their use and if they are regarded as a nuisance in the unit lines, or if only the worst of the men are selected for training as handlers. The dogs of such a battalion can be more usefully employed elsewhere.

CHAPTER VIII

PATROLLING—GENERAL

Section 1—Introduction

1. A common feature of anti-Mau Mau operations is that, irrespective of the fact that an operation has been planned at brigade or at platoon level, and whether it has been designed to:—

(a) search an area of forest,

(b) recover stolen cattle,

(c) disrupt Mau Mau food supplies,

(d) keep Mau Mau on the move,

(e) pursue a specific gang with the aid of trackers,

(f) sweep progressively a large area of forest with a large number of troops,

the troops taking part in it will almost invariably find themselves functioning in the role of a patrol which is out of visual touch wtih other troops and with a local aim of contacting and killing Mau Mau.

2. The ability to carry out skilful patrolling, which will result in contacting and killing the enemy, is therefore the prime requirement for all troops engaged in forest operations.

Section 2—Leadership and Morale

3. Since patrolling is frequently done by patrols of approximately section strength, they will often be commanded by junior N.C.O.s. These junior N.C.O.s must be well trained and their leadership qualities developed to the full before they command in the forest. Unless leadership is of the highest standard, the aim of any patrol will seldom be attained and the morale of the men will suffer accordingly.

Section 3—Briefing and De-Briefing

4. To obtain the maximum benefit from any patrol it is essential that:—

(a) The patrol commander is given definite tasks. It is quite useless to send a patrol out at short notice with no clearly defined task.

(b) Adequate preparation and planning is made by the patrol commander.

(c) The patrol is carefully and thoroughly briefed with all available information—Information gained by the local Field Intelligence Officer should in particular be made available.

(d) Information gained by the patrol is carefully checked on its return and recorded by the de-briefing officer.

5. (a) A Patrol Order Aide-Memoire which is intended to remind patrol commanders of the main points they have to cover in their orders is shown at Appendix "A" to this Chapter.

(b) A de-briefing proforma for use by all operational units is attached at Appendix "B" to this Chapter. This questionnaire should be accepted as a general guide to the types of information required from patrols. It may in addition help patrol commanders to know what is required of them as well as being of assistance for de-briefiing.

6. After briefing, a patrol commander must study maps and air photographs so thoroughly that he can make a reasonably accurate reproduction from the mental picture obtained. Whenever possible he should be given the opportunity of meeting military or civilian personnel having local knowledge of the patrol area.

7. Finally, he must appreciate the situation and make his plan before setting out on the patrol.

Section 4—Patrol Areas

8. Wherever possible a patrol commander must be given the limit and boundaries of his patrol area so that he knows the exact area of his responsibility, thereby minimising the risk of patrol clashes. These boundaries must, whenever possible, follow clear natural features, e.g. Ridges, rivers, the bamboo line or forest edge. If this is not possible it is essential that all security forces in the area (Police, K.G., etc.) are aware that operations are taking place in the area and some form of recognition signal agreed.

9. It should be made clear to patrol commanders what latitude is to be allowed, regarding boundaries, in the event of his patrol encountering fresh terrorist tracks leading out of his area.

10. Whenever possible the maximum latitude should be given to patrols to follow up unexpected encounters rather than risk losing the chance of an engagement. In practice it is almost impossible for a patrol in the forest to pinpoint its position sufficiently accurately to hand over to another unit, and in any case the delay which such a course would involve would almost certainly result in loss of contact with the terrorists. In Kenya the practice of demanding the right to enter another unit's operational area is known as "bulldozing".

11. When a patrol has been given permission to "bulldoze" should the occasion demand it, the patrol commander should make every effort to report his plans to his headquarters by wireless. If for a variety of reasons he is unable to establish communications he should nevertheless continue his action whilst remaining aware of the risk he is thus incurring of a clash with another patrol.

12. When news of a patrol "bulldozing" does reach a superior headquarters, every effort must be made to inform all other troops of that patrol's change of plan and its probable line of advance. The instruction covering the "Bulldozer" system is at Appendix "C" to this chapter.

Section 5—Size and Composition of Patrols

13. A patrol must be small enough to move silently and yet have sufficient fire power for effective offensive action. It must also be taken into account that the Mau Mau seldom stand and fight; if they do they will only increase the chances of a determined and well led patrol of inflicting casualties on them.

14. Patrols in Kenya must almost invariably be "all purpose" patrols, prepared to fight, ambush, pursue and reconnoitre. It is therefore recommended that they should be composed and armed as follows:—

```
           ←— DIRECTION OF ADVANCE

T  S   T ——— Visual ——— C  B  W  R        EY  2IC
(Recce Gp)   distance   (Aslt Gp)         (Sp Gp)

    Key:— T  Tracker        W   WS operator
           S  Scout          R   Rifleman
           C  Commander      EY  EY Rifleman
           B  Bren gunner    2IC 2nd in Command
```

Note 1. It is appreciated that there is only one EY rifle to a platoon and that not all patrols can have them.

Note 2. The group formation shown is a convenient one and will make control easier.

Note 3. The Bren Gunner is frequently located with the Support Group.

Note 4. The size of patrol recommended may appear small to carry out a successful engagement with a large gang. In fact, if the patrol brings accurate fire to bear from its wide variety of weapons the difficulty will be not to beat the enemy off but to inflict sufficient casualties before he vanishes.

Section 6—Silent Signals

15. The silent signals given in this section should be used on all patrols and on every other operation requiring complete silence.

16. The signals shown below are additional to those normally taught, i.e. advance, halt, turn about, double, etc.
  (a) *Enemy seen or suspected.*—Thumb pointed towards the ground from a clenched fist.
  (b) *No enemy in sight or All Clear or OK.*—Thumb pointed upwards from a closed fist.
  (c) *Support Group.*—The clenched fist.
  (d) *Assault Group.*—The Victory Sign.
  (e) *Recce Group.*—The clenched fist with forefinger upright.
  (f) *Section Commander.*—Two fingers held against arm to indicate Cpl's chevrons.
  (g) *Platoon Commander.*—Two fingers held on the shoulder to indicate Lieut's pips.
  (h) *You.*—Point at man concerned.
  (j) *Me.*—Indicate the chest.
  (k) *Give covering fire.*—Weapon brought into the aim.
  (i) *Track Junction.*—Arms crossed.
  (m) *House or Hut.*—Hands formed into an inverted V to indicate the shape of a roof.
  (n) *Recce.*—Hand held up to eye as though using a monocular.
  (o) *Attack.*—Clenched first swung vigorously in direction attack is required.
  (p) *Form ambush.*—Hand placed over face followed by pointing to place for ambush.

Section 7—Big Game

1. There is no doubt that big game in the Kenya forests are a more apparent danger than the Mau Mau to inexperienced troops. If the following simple facts are borne in mind, however, the apprehension of newcomers to the forest will be relieved:—
  (a) Elephant and buffalo have excellent senses of hearing and smell, and will usually move away if human beings are about.
  (b) All big game usually keep to game tracks and, therefore, provided camp is made off the game track and in thick bush, there is relatively little danger.

2. Elephant, buffalo and rhino are, however, particularly dangerous in areas which have been recently bombed. In these circumstances they frequently charge on sight and particular precautions are necessary.

3. A knowledge of the reactions of certain game animals upon scenting or encountering human beings will be of value from the operational aspect. Elephants, rhino and buffalo, should they suddenly stampede when you have not caused them to do so, the wind being in your favour, may well mean that they have seen or scented Mau Mau. Baboon, Bushbuck, Sykes Monkey, Colobus Monkey and Laurie Birds, give distinctive warning cries if they scent or see humans. Be on the watch for circling vultures, as they may well indicate a hideout where meat is left about. Hyenas calling repeatedly at night, or many hyena tracks concentrating in one direction, may also mean a hideout.

4. Do not attempt to shoot game. Army weapons are not made to kill animals, and the .303 round is not designed to penetrate through the heavy bones, hide and flesh of game. Should a patrol be charged by a big game animal it should get off the path upwind of the beast as quickly and as quietly as possible without panic. Animals, being normally more frightened of humans than humans are frightened of them, seldom charge meaningly. More often than not, so-called charges are only animals making off in all directions in blind panic. Herds of cow elephants with calves, and rhino and buffalo with calves, should however be avoided at all times by moving round them upwind.

APPENDIX "A" TO CHAPTER VIII
PATROL ORDER—AIDE-MEMOIRE
Suggested Headings

1. Aim of Patrol
2. Information
    (a) Types of country to be traversed.
    (b) Mau Mau:—
        (i) Strength.
        (ii) Weapons.
        (iii) Known or likely locations and patrol activities.

(When any accurate information available.)

(c) Own troops (including Police):—
    (i) Patrol activities of other patrols (including Tracker/Combat Teams).
    (ii) Air Force tasks if any.

3. **Plan**
    (a) Strength and composition of patrol.
    (b) Time of leaving and anticipated time of return.
    (c) Routes out and in (in general terms).
    (d) Probable bounds and RVs.
    (e) Formations.
    (f) Questions to patrol before leaving.
    (g) Deception and cover plan.
    (h) Action to be taken on meeting Mau Mau (IA Drills).
    (j) Action to be taken if patrol is ambushed.
    (k) Action to be taken if lost.

4. **Administration**
    Some of the points to be considered are:—
    (a) *Rations*:—
        (i) Type.
        (ii) Number of days.
        (iii) Emergency.
    (b) *Equipment and Dress*:—
        (i) Change of clothing or not.
        (ii) Big pack or small pack.
        (iii) Poncho cape.
        (iv) Anti-malarial equipment.
        (v) Important items such as maps, compasses and air photos.
    (c) *Avoidance of noise*:—
        (i) Equipment rattling.
        (ii) Men with coughs.

(d) *Weapons*:—

    (i) Types.

    (ii) Proportion and distribution of rifles, EY rifles, LMGs, etc.

(e) *Ammunition*:—

    (i) .303 tracer, ball, 9 mm., etc.

    (ii) Grenades, hand and rifle.

    (iii) Signal cartridges.

(f) *Medical*:—

    (i) First Field dressings and first aid kit.

    (ii) Water sterilizing tablets.

    (iii) Salt tablets.

    (iv) Paludrine.

    (v) Insect repellent.

(g) Check by personal inspection that all the above are complete and serviceable.

5. Communications

(a) *Outside patrol*:—

    (i) Wireless set.

    (ii) Verey lights.

(b) *Within patrol*:—

    (i) Silent Signals.

6. Check

(a) That all are clear on the relevant items from paragraphs 1-5 above.

(b) That all are clear on the necessity for avoiding leaving traces, e.g. paper, cigarette ends, tins, food, fires, by which enemy can follow up patrol.

APPENDIX "B" TO CHAPTER VIII
DE-BRIEFING PROFORMA FOR PATROLS

1. **General**
   - (a) Area.
   - (b) Object.
   - (c) Strength and composition.
   - (d) Duration (with times and dates).
   - (e) Route followed.

2. **Topography**
   - (a) Was the intelligence briefing accurate, if not, what inaccuracies were discovered?
   - (b) Was the map accurate, if not, what were the inaccuracies?
   - (c) Were air photographs available, if so, was the interpretation of use?
   - (d) What was the state of the tracks followed?
   - (e) Did the tracks show signs of recent use?
   - (f) Where rivers were crossed or followed, are there:—
     - (i) Any bridges, what type?
     - (ii) Fords?
     - (iii) Any recent tracks near crossing places?

3. **Hides Found**
   - (a) Map Reference.
   - (b) Was it occupied, if so by how many? If not how long evacuated?
   - (c) Total accommodation.
   - (d) Any sentry posts, if so, how were they sited?
   - (e) Any warning signals?
   - (f) Give details of entry and exit tracks.
   - (g) Was it a permanent or transit hide?
   - (h) If permanent, give details of layout.
   - (j) Any food dumps in or near the hide or any signs of cultivation?
   - (k) Any subsidiary hides?
   - (l) Any arms or ammunition found, if so, what condition and quantity?

(*m*) Any documents found, if so:—
    (i) Where were they found?
    (ii) Has the place of finding been put on each document?
    (iii) Where are they now?
(*n*) Any indication of direction of Mau Mau leaving hide?

4. **Contacts with Mau Mau**
    (*a*) Where contacted?
    (*b*) How many?
    (*c*) How were they dressed?
    (*d*) Details of arms and condition.
    (*e*) Any estimate of quantity of ammunition per man?
    (*f*) Any indication of condition of ammunition?
    (*g*) Any pointers to identification of commander?
    (*h*) Any snipers?
    (*j*) Any automatic weapon group?
    (*k*) Did they appear healthy?
    (*l*) What was their morale like?
    (*m*) Did they use bugles or any system of signals?
    (*n*) Any casualties?
        (i) Own troops.
        (ii) Mau Mau.
    (*o*) Any captured Mau Mau?
    (*p*) Any surrendered Mau Mau?
    (*q*) Have the dead Mau Mau been identified? If not
        (i) Any photographs taken?
        (ii) Any recognizable features?
    (*r*) When engagement was broken off:—
        (i) In what direction did the Mau Mau leave?
        (ii) Did they use known tracks?
        (iii) Where were you when the Mau Mau tracks were lost?

5. **Any Comments**

APPENDIX "C" TO CHAPTER VIII

BULLDOZER PROCEDURE

1. Background

In the past there have been instances of patrols (both army and police), hot on the trail of a gang, giving up the chase when the pursuing patrol has no authority.

2. Aim

The aim of the BULLDOZER procedure is to make it possible for patrols, etc., engaged in active operations, to cross operational and administrative boundaries without check and without fear or difficulty.

3. BULLDOZER

The essence of the matter is that BULLDOZER will only apply to patrols, etc., in hot pursuit. The procedure will be as follows:—

(*a*) BULLDOZER will NOT be implemented by an officer below the rank of Lt.-Col. except that it may be implemented by a field officer temporarily in command of a unit normally commanded by a Lt.-Col. and also by a field officer in command of an independent force, i.e. Rift Valley Force.

(*b*) When planning an operation which may involve troops crossing from one operational area to another the officer planning the operation will inform the Senior Army and Police Officers in the areas into which operations may extend as follows:—

WARNING ORDER (.) BULLDOZER probable (or possible) in area .... date ....
time .... direction .... strength ....
unit ....

A copy of this signal will be sent to O.C. 1340 Flight R.A.F.

(*c*) Commanding Officers will ensure that all patrols likely to be involved in BULLDOZER operations carry wireless.

(d) *When it is necessary to implement the* BULLDOZER *procedure* the officer authorized to do so will send out the following signal by fastest possible means:—

BULLDOZER (.) area .... date .... time .... direction .... strength .... unit .... This message will be sent to next higher formation (who will inform G (Ops. G.H.Q.), formation into which penetration is to be made, and R.A.F. If it is impossible to contact any of the above the message to the next higher formation will include "Please inform ...."

(e) *On receipt of a* BULLDOZER *message*

(i) The officer in command of the area into which penetration is to be made will ensure that all Army and police units in the BULLDOZER area are informed at once. The BULLDOZER message may come over the Army or Police net, responsibility for disseminating the information rests with the Army or Police Headquarters receiving the message.

(ii) 1340 Flight R.A.F. will despatch an aircraft to fly over the BULLDOZER area and, having located the BULLDOZER patrol, to report the movements of the patrol and, if possible, the gang. On receipt of this information 1340 Flight R.A.F. will keep informed the Officer in command of the area into which penetration has been made.

(f) COMMAND

Command of the operation will remain with the pursuing patrol until forces of equivalent size (or greater) have been deployed by the officer in whose area the operations are taking place. Command will then pass, at a time to be mutually arranged, by the commanders on the spot.

CHAPTER IX

PATROLLING—TACTICS

Section 1—Patrol Formation

General

1. Section 5 of Chapter VIII gives the recommended size and order of march of a patrol. It is further recommended that when the size of the patrol is increased for a specific operation the three groups, e.g. Reconnaissance, Assault and Support Groups, are still adhered to.

The enemy in Kenya only very infrequently attempts to ambush a patrol. It is seldom necessary, even when crossing open ground, to drop off the Support Group, in order to "keep one foot always on the ground". This procedure would mean slower progress and this is frequently unacceptable.

Formations

2. Patrols will almost invariably have to move in single file. Even on the moorlands the narrow tracks frequently offer the only line of advance. The Reconnaissance Group should always be in the front, followed by the Assault Group with the Support Group behind it. The gap between the Reconnaissance and Assault Groups should be the maximum visual distance in close country but in open ground the gap should not be so great that a small pebble thrown at the Reconnaissance Group will not attract their attention. The Assault and Support Groups should be together. Distances between individuals in the groups should not exceed five yards.

Position of Commanders

3. The correct place for the commander is at the head of the Assault Group. From this position he can maintain effective control, and can keep a careful watch on navigation. There are possibly two exceptions when the commander would be more correctly placed with the Reconnaissance Group:—

(a) When trackers come on to numerous fresh tracks and require continual advice as to which to follow.

(b) When the commander knows the area so well that navigation is unnecessary.

4. Many patrol commanders may plead that they are always up the front and would not consider being anywhere else. This is acceptable for the above average, but for the average commander it is impossible to navigate, observe and control the Reconnaissance Group at the same time.

Organization of Observation

5. The easiest way for the patrol to maintain all-round observation is for all but the trackers and the leading scout to number off with the odd numbers looking one way and the even numbers the other. The necessity for acute observation to the flanks must however be firmly impressed on all members of the patrol, since it is known that when Mau Mau terrorists are surprised on a track, they will move a few yards only and lie low, rather than risk detection by the noise they would make if they tried to cover a greater distance through thick undergrowth. A well-trained patrol should be able to spot the places where they have hurriedly left the track. Patrols should have one man detailed to look up to spot Mau Mau sentries hiding in trees. Finally, all men must be trained to look THROUGH foliage rather than at it.

Section 2—Fieldcraft and Movement

Tracking and Observation

6. The success of any patrol is nearly always dependent on good tracking and observation. Trackers or tracker dogs will normally lead the Reconnaissance Group. The manner in which they are handled is dealt with in Chapters VI and VII of this handbook. The whole Reconnaissance Group, however, being the eyes and ears of the patrol, must be able to give warning to the remainder, of the presence of Mau Mau or big game. They can only do this by stopping whenever the field of view is reasonable and continuously observing. When the vegetation is so thick that field of view is limited to ten yards, the sense of hearing will be the only means of warning. In these conditions the patrol should stop for two minutes every 15 minutes and listen intently in absolute silence. It cannot be sufficiently emphasized that when listening in the jungle the man who is still will always hear the man who is moving. It therefore follows that the whole time a patrol is on the move

the advantage of surprise lies with the enemy, and that whilst they are halted the chances of the patrol hearing enemy movement is increased.

All members of patrols must be taught to improve their powers of observation and what to look for. They must learn to observe every movement, sign, footprint, bruised or broken foliage and smoke. The sense of smell is much improved if smoking is prohibited, furthermore, the prohibition of smoking decreases the chance of Mau Mau scenting our patrols or detecting where they have been. Finally it is again emphasized that the Reconnaissance Group is mainly pre-occupied to the front and it is the job of every man to observe closely the flank he has been detailed to watch and to try and spot something which the others may have missed.

Silence

7. This is essential at all times. Silence here refers both to voice and movement. With practice it is possible to move at considerable speed in comparative silence. All members of patrols must learn to move steadily and carefully, to part the bamboo or undergrowth rather than crash through, and to avoid treading on dry leaves, sticks, rotten wood, etc., wherever possible. A list of silent signs in common use is at Section 6 of Chapter VIII.

Track Discipline

8. Care must be taken not to signpost the route with the slightest trace of litter such as cigarette ends, sweet papers and even the smallest scraps of waste food. All these should be kept and burned when convenient. All tins must be punctured before burying, so that they will be of no use to the Mau Mau if they are found and unearthed.

Speed of Movement

9. Timings which are normal for open warfare do not apply under conditions in Kenya. When patrolling, a speed of a mile an hour is extremely good going and distance is often calculated in hours of marching instead of miles. Speed will be obtained more by intelligent planning than by trying to push quickly and blindly forward.

Patrolling under forest conditions and particularly at high altitudes is fatiguing physically and mentally. Care must be exercised that the patrol is fresh and ready for action at all times and consideration must therefore be given to halts for rest during a patrol which is not in contact with the enemy, so that should a contact occur, a vigorous action can be fought and a vigorous pursuit conducted.

Halts

10. Whenever possible patrols should get off tracks for short halts. The whole patrol must get off the track on the same side and is then virtually in an ambush position against any enemy moving along the track. Sentries should be posted to watch each end of the track and the remainder of the patrol, whilst resting, should maintain a careful listening watch. Where it is not possible to get off the track for the short halt, sentries should be similarly posted and a bend selected so that the patrol cannot be seen by anyone approaching along the track from either direction. Insistence on the whole patrol listening during short halts will assist in reminding them of the necessity for strict silence on their own part.

Section 3—Patrol Bases

General

11. Whether a patrol is out for 24 hours or seven days it will normally be necessary for the patrol to stop and make a temporary or permanent base for use during the hours of darkness. Provided there is a drill for establishing and disbanding a base, there should be little waste of time and confusion.

Security

12. The base should whenever possible be established off the game tracks. If it is, however, found necessary to camp on a track most game can be prevented from using it if two or three members of the patrol urinate on the track about 20 yards each side of the camp. If this useful trick is not adopted there is likely to be continual interference and some danger from big game which may well necessitate the moving or even the temporary abandonment of the base during the night.

13. The halt to establish a base should be made sufficiently early to enable preparations to be completed in daylight, to avoid unnecessary noise and for cooking fires to be lit and extinguished before the onset of darkness. Fires must not be re-lit until darkness has passed. In some areas it may be necessary to use tommy cookers the whole time. When in close contact with the Mau Mau the patrol should consider the prohibition of all cooking.

14. Sentries must be posted as soon as a halt is made and every man given an alarm position. Alarm positions must be manned at dusk and dawn. Before darkness a small patrol should circle the base to make certain that no enemy are within earshot.

15. All personnel must have their weapons by them, whatever task they may be given to perform.

Siting a Base

16. The requirements differ to some extent depending upon whether the base is temporary or permanent, generally speaking, however, the following requirements apply to both:—

(a) If possible, on terrain suitable for wireless communication.

(b) Within 300 yards of water.

(c) Sheltered from the wind, if at a high altitude.

(d) Away from game tracks.

(e) On firm, dry and level ground.

Drill for Establishing Base

17.

(a) Patrol commander points out bivouac, cooking, and European and African latrine areas.

(b) Patrol splits into pairs, this allows for one of the two to be detached for a purely military task whilst the other erects their joint bivouac, cleans his personal weapon, uses the latrine, etc.

(c) *Patrol Tasks*
    (i) Sentries detailed and changed every 20 minutes during remaining hours of daylight to allow for personal tasks to be undertaken by all.
    (ii) Personnel detailed for cooking and digging latrines.
(d) Patrol commander briefs patrol for following day and issues orders to include such items as:—
    (i) Sentries, passwords, stand-to, stand-down and alarm scheme.
    (ii) Local patrolling.
    (iii) Wireless.
    (iv) Water.
    (v) Cooking, fires, smoking.
    (vi) Latrines, urinals and refuse.
    (vii) Work required the next day for maintenance or closing down of base.

Sentries

18. By Day

It will often be impossible to cover all the tracks near the base. Sentries must be just out of earshot of the few sounds which are unavoidable in preparing a base. They should normally be armed with automatic weapons. A silent method of warning the base must be arranged. A piece of string tied to the leg of the cook, or any other member of the base who is sitting down, is one solution.

19. By Night

The bivouac area should be as compact as possible so that only one double sentry post need be manned. This post should be close to the bivouacs. A prowler sentry is not advised, as the noise of his movement will give away the position of the base to any listener and at the same time prevent our own sentries from listening for enemy movement. Sentries should have at least one automatic weapon between them and a torch each. Verey pistols are not recommended owing to the unreliability of the cartridges and the risk of downward richochet off overhanging branches.

Conclusion

20. A commander must appreciate that even though a base is established for only one night, it must be efficiently organized and run.

An efficient base is one in which:—

(a) The security arrangements are sound and known to all.
(b) Duties are evenly distributed and notified in time to allow men to make their own administration arrangements.
(c) The organizing of rest and washing is clear-cut and sufficient within operational demands.
(d) The cooking and sanitation routine is well organized and is of as high a standard as possible.
(e) A high standard of discipline is maintained.
(f) The members have been previously practised in carrying out their various tasks so that these can be performed with the minimum of noise.

Section 4—Return to Base Drill

21. A sound drill must be worked out for the patrol when it returns to base. The men will be tired, hungry, thirsty and dirty. Points to be considered are:—

(a) Clearing of weapons by patrol commander.
(b) De-briefing on important points requiring immediate action.
(c) Handing in of patrol stores.
(d) Cleaning of weapons.
(e) Personal washing and hygiene.
(f) Mail and N.A.A.F.I. supplies.
(g) Pay.
(h) Rest.
(i) Full de-briefing—full discussion on mistakes.

22. A de-briefing *pro forma* is given at Appendix "B" to Chapter VIII.

Section 5—Conclusion

23. Patrolling is a vital task for the infantry soldier at all times. Here in Kenya it occupies the greater part of his time. Sound knowledge of fieldcraft, Mau Mau tactics, navigation and the necessary I.A. drills is required to ensure that the patrol will work smoothly. When not operating against the Mau Mau, the various aspects of patrolling including shooting from the shoulder, should be continually practised. These measures are certain to increase the success of patrols and by this means more than any other, morale and keenness will be kept up and hence the high standard of patrolling maintained.

CHAPTER X

AMBUSHES

Section 1—General

1. In most respects ambushes in Kenya are similar to those in any other theatre. The two main differences are as follows:—

(a) Up to time of writing the Mau Mau have not been as active as might have ben expected in laying ambushes for the security forces. The emphasis in this Chapter will therefore be on the technique of laying ambushes rather than on how to deal with enemy ambushes.

(b) The standard of fieldcraft by Mau Mau forest gangs is very high and great care is therefore necessary on the part of security forces if their own ambushes are to succeed. In the past many otherwise well-planned ambushes have failed because of careless track discipline or noise.

Section 2—Forest Ambushes

2. **Laid by Mau Mau.**—The IA drill for an encircling attack on a Mau Mau ambush is given in Chapter XIII, Section 3.

3. **Laid by Security Forces.**—The following normal points must be noted with particular stress on sub-paragraphs (iv) and (v):—

(i) Careful planning and briefing are essential.

(ii) Any African seen to observe the approach of the ambush party must be detained until the ambush is discounted.

(iii) Positions must be sited to give cover to the ambush party yet afford a reasonable field of fire.

(iv) Great care must be taken, when taking up positions, to leave no tell-tale tracks and other signs of occupation which will serve as warning to approaching Mau Mau.

(v) Complete silence and lack of movement must be maintained in the ambush position.

(vi) Clear orders must be issued regarding the springing of the ambush to ensure that everyone opens fire at exactly the right time. The greatest danger is that fire will be opened prematurely. The only occasion when it is acceptable for an ambush to be sprung other than by the prearranged means is when a member of the ambush party sees that the enemy have spotted the ambush and are turning back. In these circumstances he should open fire immediately and without orders. Provision for this circumstance must be included in the commanders initial orders.

(vii) Good fire discipline is also essential so that fire can be stopped at once to allow the enemy to be followed up.

(viii) Weapons must be laid in the exact positions in which they are required to fire.

(ix) Sentries must have string connected to the commanders wrist so that they can give silent warning of the enemy's approach.

(x) Trip flares should be prepared for operation by the patrol commander on night ambushes. These flares should be sited to light up the killing area yet shielded from the eyes of the ambush party by tree trunks or bushes.

(xi) Other troops and Police in the area must be informed of the ambush. If necessary local Kikuyu Guard must be confined to their posts if there is a danger of their approaching the ambush.

Section 3—Road Ambushes

4. As previously implied, there have so far been very few cases when the Mau Mau have laid road ambushes, and at the time of publication of this handbook there is no need for vehicles to travel in pairs, or for any special anti-ambush precaution. Everyone should, however, be alert at all times and be capable of opening fire immediately while driving through the operational area. If vehicles are carrying troops the tarpaulin covers should normally be down to enable them to return fire with all available weapons.

5. Vigilance is particularly necessary in road movement by night, since although full-scale ambushes are rare, shots are sometimes fired by night at passing vehicles.

6. If the enemy changes his habits and starts to lay road ambushes, orders will be issued for vehicles to travel in pairs in the operational areas and for all troops to be practised in aggressive counter-ambush drills.

CHAPTER XI

DRILL FOR ATTACKING A HIDE ON INFORMATION

Section 1—General

1. It is very difficult to lay down a uniform drill for a pre-planned attack on a hide which will apply on all occasions, because Mau Mau tactics and the types of location used for hides vary considerably from area to area.

2. The drill suggested in this Chapter can, however, easily be amended to suit different circumstances, and can be used as a basis for initial planning on those few occasions when information from air photographs, prisoners or informers points conclusively to an occupied hide being at a certain place. If the operation is undertaken on the information of an informer, it should be carried out as early as possible, as gangs move their hides when they suspect a breach of security. The interrogator should endeavour to discover the whereabouts of the gangs alternative hide, their emergency RV, or at least the most likely direction of escape.

3. On every occasion there is, however, a requirement for four tactical groups of troops, all of which can normally be found from a rifle company. All plans should normally be based on the correct use of these groups whose suggested composition and roles are given below:—

(a) *The assault group*

The aim of bringing the maximum fire power to bear on the hide must be balanced against the difficulty of moving too large a body of men through the forest without alerting the enemy. The assault group should therefore consist of about eight men who have proved themselves masters of silent movement, armed with a high proportion of LMGs, SMCs and an EY rifle. The task of the assault group will be to approach as near as possible to the hide undetected and to open fire on its occupants with every available weapon. The suggested detailed composition of the assault group is given in Appendix "A".

(b) *The Follow-up Group*

Since a proportion of the occupants of a hide will always survive the initial burst of fire and make for the cover of the forest, it is essential to have a Follow-up Group, which has not been tied down by the initial fire fight, to take up the pursuit. If a Tracker/Combat Team can be made available, it would be ideally suited to this purpose. Failing this, the Follow-up Group should be a normal patrol of about nine men augmented by native trackers and both types of war-dog if available. The task of the Follow-up Group will be to close on the hide as soon as fire has been opened, to pick up the most promising tracks and follow them. The suggested detailed composition of a Follow-up Group is given in Appendix "A".

(c) *The Support Group*

Since the Assault Group must consist entirely of fighting troops, a small Support Group must be at hand to provide them at the earliest opportunity with wireless communication, medical aid, an interrogator if one can be made available, and the heavier part of their equipment which will have been discarded before the final approach. The suggested composition of the Support Group is given in Appendix "A".

(d) *Stops*

These must be put out to cover all likely escape routes from the hide. They should be at such a distance from the hide as will not prejudice the secrecy of the operation.

Air Support

4. In addition to the four tactical groups described above it will be a great asset to the operation if a light aircraft can be timed to arrive over the hide after fire has been opened. The most suitable time is likely to be at sunrise, by which time the Assault Group will have started the engagement.

5. Should air support be available all tactical groups and the headquarters of the operation should be equipped with No. 88 W.S. for ground/air communication.

Section 2—Sequence of Action

6. The main factor to be borne in mind is that Mau Mau sentries are extremely good, and by day it will be extremely difficult to get past them. A study of Mau Mau habits has revealed the following facts:—

(a) *Positioning of Sentries*

(i) Usually sentries are posted at short intervals on the main tracks between the Mau Mau hideout in the forest and the forest edge.

(ii) Most gangs do not post sentries along paths behind their camps.

(iii) Sentries are posted early in the morning until late evening.

(iv) Sentries are not normally posted at night. If they are they are in close proximity to the camp, and are probably not very alert.

(b) *Duties of the Sentries*

(i) As soon as the security forces are seen, the sentry on the forest edge warns the next sentry along the path. This warning is carried on to the gang by one sentry after the other.

(ii) The method of warning varies:—

(1) By striking bamboo.

(2) By running to the next sentry and telling him the news.

(3) By various animal calls.

(c) *Conclusion*

It will be seen that to approach a Mau Mau hide direct from the Reserve is well nigh impossible if the sentries are alert. The method of approach, which has been found most successful, is by moving the assaulting troops into the forest by night or under thick cover along river valleys, well to the flank of the hide which it is proposed to attack, and to move down towards the Mau Mau hideouts from the side where there are unlikely to be sentries. The stops must move initially to an area below the hide and well to a flank and take up their stop positions after sentries have been withdrawn.

7. The following sequence of action and timings are therefore recommended.

D-1

During late evening the company moves into forest (if not already there) using the thick cover of river valleys and keeping well to a flank of the believed location of the hide. Stops move towards their positions after giving Mau Mau sentries ample time to withdraw. Assault Group, Follow-up Group and Support Group move to a position approximately 1,700 yards above the hide.

Night D-1/D Day

Assault Group, Follow-up Group and Support Group, in this order, move to within striking distance but well out of earshot of the hide. Stops move into their positions if the terrain allows this manœuvre during darkness.

D Day

(a) Stops use the 30 minutes or so of twilight after first light to get into their final positions.

(b) Assault Group uses these 30 minutes to get into an assault position on the hide.

(c) Informers or P.O.W., trackers and escorting rifleman dropped off just short of hide.

(d) Assault Group fan out as far as possible.

(e) Fire opened on orders of commander.

(f) Follow-up Group move straight forward, select most promising tracks and carry out pursuit.

(g) Support Group meet up with Assault Group.

(h) Wireless Operator opens up communications to Officer i/c Stops and Battalion Headquarters.

(j) Mopping up and thorough searching of hide.

(k) Casualties and prisoners evacuated, interrogation where applicable.

(l) Formation of Assault Group into a second Follow-up Group with elements of Support Group and dispatch on tracking patrol.

Section 3—The Assault

8. The aim of the assault is to kill the maximum number of Mau Mau with the initial opening of fire. The Assault Group should therefore be deployed as compactly as possible and within visual distance. If the Assault Group is split there is a danger that fire will not be opened simultaneously and our own troops may shoot each other. Furthermore, the additional movement round the hide will increase chances of detection by the enemy. The recommended positioning of the Assault Group is shown diagrammatically in Appendix "B" to this Chapter.

9. As soon as the initial bursts of fire have been opened the Assault Group must move in on the hide with the possible exception of the two flanking men who should, if the terrain allows it, take up fire positions to prevent any enemy breaking out to a flank. A number of seven-second grenades fired from an EY rifle, the first being fired at the moment of the initial opening of fire and aimed beyond the far side of the hide, will tend to close the fourth side of the "box". The object of these grenades is not so much to kill the enemy as to make them hesitate if they take this line of escape and present the firers of the automatic weapons with further targets.

10. The task of the Assault Group must be clearly defined. This task is to destroy all the enemy in the hide and its immediate vicinity and to mop up in and around the hide only. They will otherwise be tempted to disperse in all directions after a different quarry and leave the job of mopping-up undone. The task of carrying out the pursuit is that of the Follow-up Group.

11. After the mopping-up is completed, prisoners have been marshalled, the wounded treated and the whole vicinity thoroughly searched for weapons, the Commander may form a second Follow-up Group from the Assault Group and elements of the Support Group. If he decides to do this, additional trackers, wireless and dogs, if available, will be included in the Support Group.

Section 4—The Follow-up

12. Whenever Mau Mau are surprised in large numbers by determined action on the part of the security forces they disperse as individuals and run as hard as they can away from the scene of action. They normally have a pre-arranged meeting place

against such an eventuality at a distance which varies considerably according to the terrain and the gang's tactics. A track diagram would therefore show a number of individual tracks radiating out in all directions but eventually converging together until they all reach one place. This may be either a rendezvous, a temporary hide or an alternative hide. If it is the latter it is likely to be a considerable distance from the original hide.

13. It follows from the above that the trackers and dogs of the Follow-up Group have only to follow one track, and unless they are unlucky enough to follow the tracks of a wounded man who dies or the one gangster who gets lost, this track will eventually lead to the re-assembled remnants of the gang.

14. The aim of the Follow-up Group is to pick up the best set of tracks after the assault, to re-establish contact with the gang and to engage it. If tracking were a simpler art, if conditions of climate and terrain did not intervene and if the Mau Mau were less skilful in covering up their tracks, a high percentage of re-engagements would be the rule. The fact that they are comparatively rare is due mainly to the above factors but also in part to a lack of basic realization on the part of many junior leaders of the combined tracking potential of good native trackers and dogs. A skilful interchange of the use of these two types of trackers in accordance with the variations of ground surface and light, coupled with the determination to engage the enemy at all costs, will materially increase the chances of such an engagement.

15. It is for the above reason that a Tracker/Combat Team is recommended for the follow-up role after an assault, as the commanders of these teams have had special training in the use of trackers and war dogs and in many cases have learnt some part of the art of tracking on their own account.

Section 5—The Support Group

The function of the Support Group is described in Section 1, paragraph 3 (c) of this Chapter. The suggested composition is given in detail in Appendix "A".

Section 6—Stops

General

16. If the attack on a hide is mounted by a company there will be an equivalent strength of two platoons available for use as stops. If the information points to the gang being extremely large, these may well be augmented by additional troops.

Positions

17. Stops should be put out covering all likely routes from the hide. They should not normally be more than three miles from the hide or the perimeter to be held will be too long. They should not, however, be less than about one mile from the hide or the secrecy of the operation may be prejudiced. Every unit has its share of boneheads and butter-fingers and, since the company commander will have weeded these out of the mobile groups, they will be present in full strength amongst the stops. A further reason why the line of stops should not be too near the hide is that the Mau Mau, when surprised, scatter blindly through the forest for distances of up to half a mile, only returning to tracks when they consider that they have shaken off the immediate pursuit. Stops would have little chance of engaging the enemy under the conditions of visibility obtaining off tracks.

18. The positions of all stops must be in clearly defined places because:—

   (a) The initial approach to them will be made in darkness and there will be little more than half an hour of daylight to complete the final move into position.

   (b) Stop commanders must be able to find them readily.

   (c) Follow-up patrols must know when they get near them.

Section 7—Summary

19. The successful conduct of the operation which has been described in this Chapter will depend upon a large number of factors, some of which are outside the control of the troops taking part:—

   (a) The information must be correct.

   (b) The Assault Group must succeed in timing their final approach during the vital minutes when there is sufficient light to move but the sentries are not in position.

(c) The approach march of all tactical groups must be made without being seen by any messengers or food carriers who happen also to be moving in the vicinity of the hide.

(d) A high standard of silence must be maintained throughout the operation by all troops, including those acting as stops.

(e) The night navigation in the forest must be extremely accurate.

(f) The standard of marksmanship of the Assault Group must be such that the maximum casualties are inflicted in the moments of initial surprise.

(g) The final approach of the assault group must be completely noiseless. If one member of this group allows a sound to pass his lips or places a foot carelessly, the whole operation is likely to fail and the entire efforts of all the troops taking part wasted.

APPENDIX "A" TO CHAPTER XI

1. Suggested Composition of Assault Group and Weapons Carried

Role	Rank	Weapon	Remarks
Commander	Subaltern	Patchett or Sten	Commands centre fire group in assault.
2 i/c and Right Fire Group Commander	Sergeant	Patchett or Sten	Commands Right fire group in assault.
Left Fire Group Commander	Sergeant or Corporal	Patchett or Sten	Commands Left fire group in assault.
EY Rifleman	Private	EY Rifle	⎧ Ranks may well be
Bren Gunner	,,	Bren	⎨ varied to include men
Bren Gunner	,,	,,	⎬ who have been proved
Bren Gunner	,,	,,	⎩ in fieldcraft.

2. Suggested Composition of Follow-up Group and Weapons Carried

	Role	Rank	Weapon	Remarks
H.Q. and Tracking Element	Commander	Subaltern	Patchett or Sten	—
	Tracker	Civilian	Shotgun or Rifle	
	Tracker	Civilian	Shotgun or Rifle	
	Scout	Private	Patchet or Sten	
	Dog Handler	N.C.O. or Private	Revolver	V. & R. handler [of Tracker Dog.
	Dog Handler	Private	Revolver	Infantry handler of Patrol Dog.
	WS operator	Private	No. 5 Rifle	Carries set.
Combat Element	2 i/c	Sergeant	Patchett or Sten	Commands "combat" element.
	Bren gunner	Private	Bren	
	Rifleman	Private	No. 5 Rifle	
	,,	,,	,,	
	,,	,,	,,	
	,,	,,	,,	
	,,	,,	,,	

3. Suggested Composition of Support Group and Weapons Carried

	Role	Rank	Weapon	Remarks
H.Q. Element	Commander	C.S.M.	Patchett or Sten	
	WS operator	Private	No. 5 Rifle	Carries No. 46 WS.
	Medical Orderly	—	—	Carries First Aid Kit.
	Interrogator	—	—	Police or Kenya Regiment.
	Porters as required			
Attached to Support Group, if available, to enable Assault Group to be converted into a second Follow-up Group	Dog Handler	—	Revolver	V. & R. handler of Tracker Dog.
	,,	Private	Revolver	Infantry handler of Patrol Dog.
	WS operator	,,	No. 5 Rifle	Carries No. 88 Set.

APPENDIX "B" TO CHAPTER XI
DIAGRAM 1
Position of Assault Group Before Opening Fire

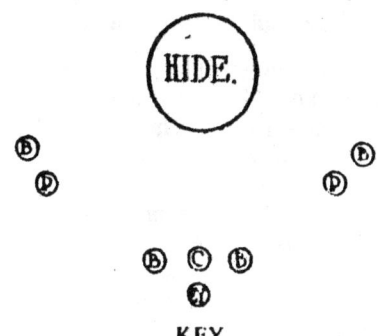

KEY

(C) Commander (Patchett). (P) Patchett.
(B) Bren gunner. (EY) EY Rifleman

DIAGRAM 2
Position of All Tactical Groups Before Opening Fire
STOPS
(Distance from Hide not to scale.)

Assault Group.

Follow Up Group.

Support Group.

CHAPTER XII

SWEEPS

Section 1—Introduction

1. Experience has shown that, because of the difficulties involved in control and direction keeping, sweeps are very rarely successful in the forest. Their value has usually been very small in comparison with the number of troops required.

2. This chapter should therefore be read with particular regard to the settled areas and reserves.

3. Principles.—The following must be observed if the sweep is to have any chance of success:—

(a) Good security.

(b) There must be sufficient troops for the task.

(c) The area to be swept must be kept small (a very common mistake is to try and sweep too large an area for the force available).

(d) Good control (which also implies good communications).

(e) Clear orders.

(f) A rate of advance which ensures a **thorough** search of the ground.

Section 2—Organization

4. The available forces must be divided into three groups:—

(a) Stop party
(b) Sweep party   } All under a single commander.
(c) Reserves.

Section 3—Stop Parties

5. Stop parties must be able to provide a high rate of accurate fire and should therefore normally be found by the Army, rather than by the Police or Kikuyu Guard.

6. **Siting—**

(a) Stops should be within visual distance of each other but must be concealed from anyone flushed by the sweeping party.

(b) It must be possible for the area between stops to be covered by fire.

(c) Stops will normally be placed on three sides of the area to be swept.

(d) Stop lines must be denoted by clear unmistakable features.

7. **Composition.**—Stops will be small and each should therefore include an automatic weapon. Each stop should be commanded by an N.C.O.

8. **Method of Operation—**

(a) Stops must move to their positions by a covered route to avoid being seen to arrive and must remain concealed on arrival. Any Africans met *en route* to stop positions must be detained until the end of the operation.

(b) To avoid disclosing the positions of stops, stray individuals who try to break the stop-line should, if possible, be detained silently.

(c) On arrival of the sweeping party, stops should stand up and give the pre-arranged recognition signal.

9. **Discipline.**—This must be strict, particularly as stops will be spread out and often out of sight and hearing of an officer. Stops must be ready for instant action throughout the operation, and all noise, smoking and fires forbidden.

Section 4—Sweep Parties

10. If available, it is often desirable to get the Kikuyu Guard backed by Police, to provide the sweep parties, as the numbers required are large.

11. **Method of Operation.**—The aim of the sweep is, of course, to ensure that the area is so well searched that no one can remain undetected in it. The sweep party should therefore advance in line of sub-units, the distance between these depending on the terrain.

12. The following points must be noted:—

(a) Kikuyu Guard have been found to flag and lose formation if the length of sweep is too long. To avoid this troops and Kikuyu Guard should be intermingled. It should be rare for the total length of a sweep to be more than 3,000 yards from start to finish.

(b) *Flexibility*

(i) The density of the swept area will vary across its length and breadth, some terrain will be open and require relatively few seachers, while other terrain, including copses, cultivation (*shambas*) and huts, will necessitate a much closer search. All commanders must be able to concentrate their forces, or part of them, to carry out particular tasks.

(ii) It follows therefore that the sweep should not merely consist of an evenly spaced line of individuals, but rather of a line of sub-units each carrying out a specific task. Report lines in particular will provide commanders with a chance to allot tasks and to redeploy their forces.

(c) Troops, police and Kikuyu Guard will always tend to follow the easiest routes, and strict supervision will be needed to ensure that thick bushes, etc., are well searched.

(d) Trees and holes in the ground must be examined, the latter particularly in bracken and maize crops. The enemy is very cunning at hiding himself and every possible hiding place must be searched, however unlikely.

(e) Sweeps should, if possible, be done in two lines of sub-units at least 200 yards apart. If this is the case the first line must never fire to its rear.

(f) Report lines will be necessary if the sweep is anything but a very short one. These should be on clearly defined features. The sweep should not stop at report lines any longer than is necessary to reform or redeploy; on no account must troops be allowed to treat the check on a report line as a rest halt.

(g) The rate of advance must be kept sufficiently slow to ensure that a proper search is made; the exact rate will naturally depend on the terrain. If limited by time it is better to search a small area thoroughly than a larger one superficially.

(h) The sweep party must be ready to engage a fleeting target immediately it appears. Personnel must therefore carry their weapons at the ready. Commanders down to section level must know which sub-units are to their flanks and to their front and rear.

13. **Weapons.**—A normal scale of arms is needed including a proportion of E.Y. rifles and grenades (including phosphorus).

Section 5—Reserves

14. Two types of reserves are desirable when carrying out a sweep.

(a) *Normal Reserve.*—To engage and destroy any Mau Mau who offer organized resistance inside the area being swept.

(b) *Follow-up.* To follow up and destroy any parties of enemy who break through the stop line.

15. **Normal Reserve.**—The commander should, whenever possible, have a reserve force, well armed with automatic weapons, E.Y. rifles and two-inch mortars, under his personal command and located near him, to deal with any gang which may give serious and prolonged resistance. The size of this force will depend on the size of the total force taking part, and on the degree of resistance expected.

16. **Follow-up Role.**—The ideal is to have a patrol, similar in composition to a tracker/combat team (see Chapter V), in the middle of each side of the area being swept, to follow-up and destroy any gangs which may escape from the area. If there are insufficient troops to permit the commander to cover every side of the swept area in this fashion, he should deploy his follow-up troops covering the most likely escape routes.

Section 6—General

17. **Aircraft.**—A spotter aircraft is invaluable and will normally be available. It can help our forces to maintain direction, as well as spotting enemy movement. It must be in wireless communication with the commander of the operation, with both sweep and stop parties, and with the reserve when deployed.

18. **Recognition**—

(*a*) A recognition signal must be decided upon beforehand and known to everyone taking part.

(*b*) All Africans taking part must wear a distinctive coloured hat and armband, which must only be distributed immediately before the operation, or it may be compromised.

19. **Reconnaissance.**—It may be necessary to dispense with reconnaissance as the sight of officers, or of any white men, may be enough to warn the enemy of the operation.

20. **Security.**—It is not always possible to guarantee 100 per cent loyalty from members of the Kikuyu Guard as certain Mau Mau members may have deliberately infiltrated into their ranks. They should therefore not be given orders for the operation until immediately before it takes place. (*See also* paragraph 18 (*b*) above.)

21. **Communications.**—The commander must have a forward control net as well as a rear link to his unit or brigade headquarters. The latter should be a 19, 22 or 62 set.

22. **Forward Control.**—This will be a VHF, 46 or 88 set on the lines of the diagram opposite.

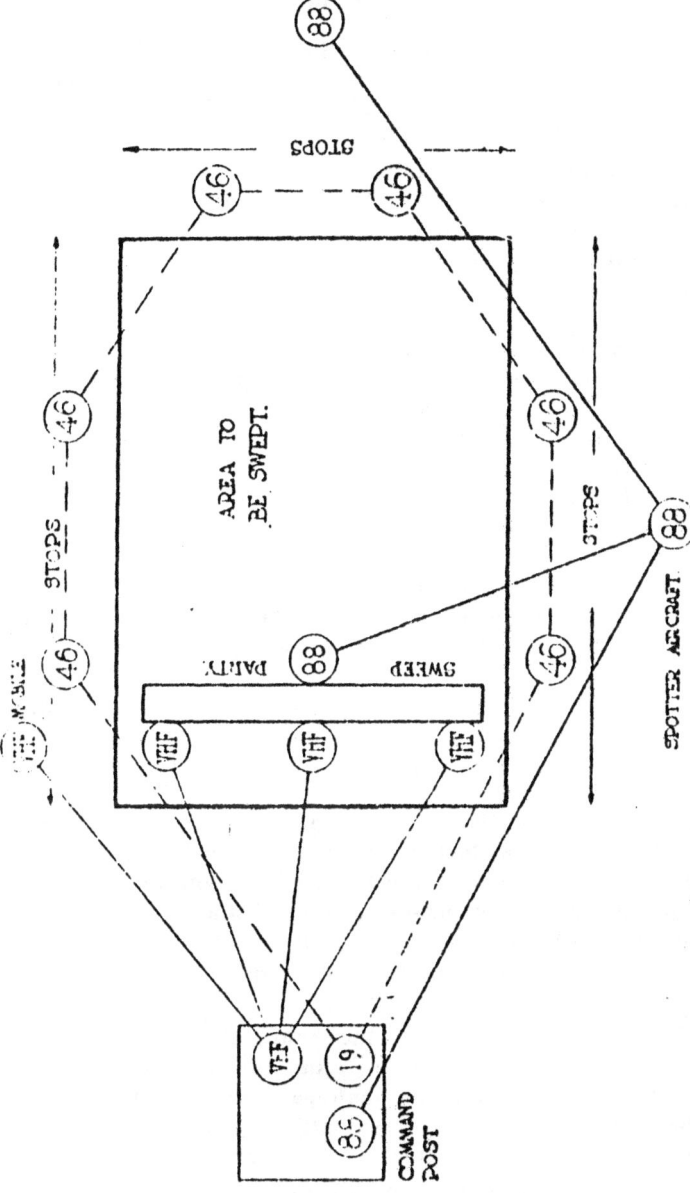

Section 7—Sweeps in the Forest

23. **General.**—The correct method of searching an area of forest is by a carefully controlled series of patrols, including the maximum number of native trackers.

24. **Method of Operation.**—The unit or sub-unit headquarters controlling the operation must set up a base either above or below the area to be swept. The deciding factor is whether wireless communication to the platoons concerned will be better from above or below.

25. The area to be swept is searched in a series of co-ordinated operations. Each company or platoon is allotted a series of areas to search in accordance with a timed programme. The area which a platoon can search in one day will depend on the terrain. As a rough guide two map squares (2,000 by 1,000 yards) has been found the maximum area which a platoon can search effectively.

26. Each platoon must establish its own base each day and the platoon commander must organize patrols of approximately section strength to search the area allocated to him.

27. **Wireless.**—If the sweep is a battalion operation, control may be in the form of a normal battalion wireless net to companies, each company having its own forward net. Owing to the fickleness of wireless sets in the forests it has, however, been found on occasion that company headquarters, though near their platoons, are in fact out of wireless touch with them. In these circumstances it has sometimes been found more satisfactory to control all the platoons on the battalion net, the battalion's forward control set having been sited on a prominent feature which can dominate the whole area of operations.

28. **Trackers.**—Owing to the restricted visibility in the forest, patrols must concentrate more on searching for Mau Mau signs and tracks than on the hope of seeing them in person in the first instance. A high standard of fieldcraft is therefore required and every native tracker available must be allocated to the platoons taking part in the operation.

CHAPTER XIII

IMMEDIATE ACTION DRILLS

Section 1—Introduction

1. Encounters with the Mau Mau are usually unexpected and the ensuing action extremely brief. It is therefore essential for patrols to be thoroughly trained in Immediate Action Drills so that patrol commanders are not forced to waste precious seconds in giving out orders. Provided that patrol commanders have a simple word to describe each tactical move, their freedom of action is in no way impaired and control is enhanced and speeded up rather than restricted.

2. For Immediate Action Drills to be effective they must be frequently practised. Before taking out a patrol the commander must also ensure that any newcomers such as dog handlers, guides, medical orderlies, etc., are fully briefed and know exactly what to do in each set of circumstances.

Section 2—IA Drills Required

3. Four IA Drills are taught as a guide. These are considered sufficient for use in the varied terrain of Kenya and they can be used in any formation.
  1. Encircling Attack and anti-Ambush drill.
  2. Immediate Ambush.
  3. Immediate Assault.
  4. Drill when unexpectedly encountering a hide.

Section 3—Encircling Attack

4. The present enemy, unlike the normal enemy encountered by British Forces, is seldom prepared to stand and fight. It is therefore logical that this drill is unlikely to be required except when caught by an enemy ambush.

5. It facilitates the speed with which the encircling attack can be put into effect if troops are trained to recognize likely Mau Mau ambush positions and the type of ground they select for their ambushes and also if troops have learnt to recognize the type of fire they will hear if they do run into an ambush.

DIAGRAM "A" ENCIRCLING ATTACK

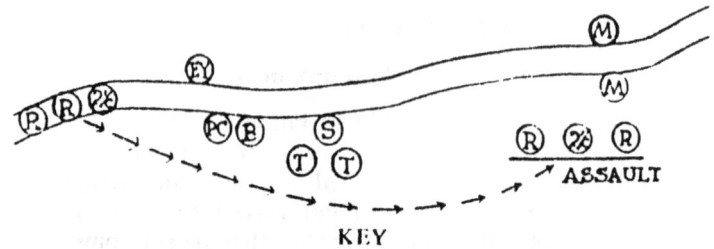

KEY

(B) Bren.
(R) Rifleman.
(EY) EY Rifleman.
(T) Trackers.

(PC) Patrol Commander.
(2 i/c) Second in Command.
(S) Scout (Reconnaissance Group).
(M) Mau Mau.

NOTES ON DIAGRAM

1. Dotted Line indicates route taken by members of the patrol who are not pinned to the ground in the opening bursts of fire.
2. Positions of patrol members when they are formed up ready to assault are shown underlined.
3. Survivors of the leading group/groups fire back at the enemy after moving their positions. It is always necessary that this leading group should be a tactical bound ahead of the Patrol Commander.
4. This drill can be worked in reverse if enemy allow the leading elements of a column to pass and take on the rear elements.
5. The time taken to encircle will vary according to the thickness of the jungle and the extent of the enemy position but will rarely be less than ten minutes.
6. Commanders select the direction of movement for their assault according to the nature of the ground.

Section 4—Immediate Ambush

6. There will be occasions when a patrol, without being seen itself, sights a Mau Mau party approaching either on the same track, or across a clearing, or in jungle. This is most likely to occur when the patrol has halted and the enemy is on the move. It is obviously advantageous to allow the Mau Mau to approach as close as possible before opening fire on them. If our own patrol is on the move there may be time only for a silent signal to be passed through the patrol, to move quietly and quickly into the positions indicated and for the signal to open fire to be given when the Mau Mau reach the position in which they are most vulnerable.

Essential are:—

(a) Discipline to ensure that no shot is fired in the excitement of the moment when Mau Mau are first sighted.
(b) Understood silent signals.
(c) Quick and silent movement and concealment.
(d) Control by the Commander, who will normally spring the ambush.

DIAGRAM "B" IMMEDIATE AMBUSH

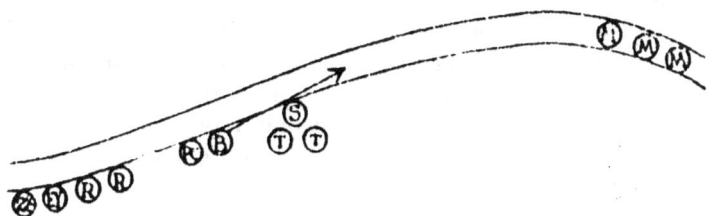

KEY

(B) Bren. (PC) Patrol Commander.
(EY) Rifleman. (2 i/c) Second in Command.
(R) Rifleman. (S) Scout.
(T) Tracker. (M) Mau Mau.

NOTES ON DIAGRAM

1. This is a drill that can be used only when the enemy is moving towards the patrol.
2. (a) The leading scout passes a silent signal back as soon as he sees the enemy approaching and the section commander then signals for Immediate Ambush (again silent).

   (b) In some cases (as when the Mau Mau are very close before the leading scout sees them) there may not be time for this. The patrol commander must, therefore, be prepared to delegate to the leading scout the responsibility for giving the silent "immediate Ambush" signal.
3. On seeing this signal the leading group must get under cover from view and remain still if they have not assumed a good fire position. The enemy may be too close to allow sufficient time for their positions to be adjusted.
4. Other groups further down the column will have more time to choose good positions and the success of the ambush will depend on the Bren being well sited.
5. The signal to open fire will normally be given by the Patrol Commander, who should be able to see when the Bren gun has a good target. Nevertheless everyone must be ready to open fire if the enemy become aware of the ambush before the signal has been given.
6. There must be a prearranged signal to cease fire. Men should remain in position until ordered to move by the Patrol Commander.

Section 5—Immediate Assault

7. This drill is used when our troops and the Mau Mau become aware of each other's presence at the same time or when the terrorists see us first. It does NOT apply when we are surprised by an ambush, when the encircling attack is the correct drill.

8. The aim is to get as many men as possible into a position from which they can shoot at the enemy. The sequence of action is as follows:—

    (a) The scout will open fire immediately at the enemy.

    (b) Trackers drop off to LEFT and RIGHT of the track.

    (c) Assault Group sprints forward under control of commander engaging every possible target with fire.

    (d) EY rifleman fires a grenade at maximum range beyond the enemy.

9. The patrol commander must control the distance to which the assault is allowed to proceed; usually if the enemy are not caught in the first 200-300 yards they are unlikely to be caught at all.

Section 6—Immediate Assault on Terrorist Camps

10. It is extremely unlikely that a patrol will encounter an occupied hide by day without first bumping a sentry. The sentry will either fire a shot at the patrol to warn the occupants of the hide or, if he has spotted the patrol without having himself been seen, he will most likely slip away and warn the occupants of the hide who will immediately disperse.

11. There are therefore three sets of circumstances with which to contend:—

    (a) The sentry spots the patrol first and slips back to the hide.—The patrol will in this case be unaware of his action and will eventually come upon an unoccupied hide.

    (b) The patrol spot the sentry without themselves being seen.—In this case the commander has a chance of preparing a plan of attack to suit the circumstances and terrain.

    (c) Recognition is mutual and the sentry fires a warning shot.—It is on this occasion that there is no time to lose and an IA Drill is essential.

12. The basis of the IA Drill is the immediate deployment of the maximum fire power available. Sequence of action should be as follows:—

    (a) Trackers drop off to each side of track.

    (b) Scout fires at sentry if a reasonable target is presented.

    (c) Scout doubles at full speed up the approach to the hide followed by commander, the Bren gunner and remainder of assault group.

    (d) On reaching hide scout bears to the RIGHT, Bren gunner bears to the LEFT, commander remains in centre.

    (e) Fire is opened by all concerned at all targets which present themselves.

    (f) EY rifleman, if included in the patrol, fires grenades at maximum range on the far side of the hide.

    (g) Remaining fighting members of the patrol bear RIGHT or LEFT on orders from the commander and as the situation dictates.

13. It is not possible to lay down in detail how the remainder of the action should be fought. The purpose of the IA Drill is to ensure that the assault is instantaneous and fast and that on arrival at the hide, both flanks are automatically covered and the far side bombed with grenades.

CHAPTER XIV
AIR OPERATIONS
Section 1—General

Introduction

1. This chapter is intended to give a working knowledge first of the types of air operations undertaken by the R.A.F. and Kenya Police Reserve Air Wing in support of the security forces and, secondly, of how this support can be called for by units.

Air Strength Available

2. The following types of R.A.F. aircraft are available:—

Type	Armament or Task
Lincolns	14 x 500 lb. .5 H.M.G.s
Harvards	8 x 20 lb. .303 M.G.
Meteors	Photography
Austers	Speech broadcasting
Sycamore Helicopter	Casualty evacuation

The Lincolns and Harvards are the striking force and are the aircraft which meet the day-to-day offensive requirements. For specific operations of importance Vampire and Valletta aircraft from Aden or Middle East may be called upon to supplement this force.

3. The more intimate air support necessitated by the characteristics of the country and the peculiarities of the Emergency is met by the Tri Pacers of the Kenya Police Reserve Air Wing. These light aircraft can carry a maximum of three passengers, 200/300 lb. of supplies or a small number of 20-lb. bombs.

4. All operational elements of the R.A.F. are based at R.A.F., Eastleigh. The Kenya Police Air Wing is located at Nairobi West with flights at Mweiga and Nakuru.

(a) Ground Liaison Officers are deployed at R.A.F., Eastleigh, and at Mweiga. Their duties are:—

    (i) To keep the operating air forces in the military picture.

    (ii) To interpret the ground forces air support requirements and brief air crews.

    (iii) To collect and transmit to interested formations all military information gleaned from air crews.

(*b*) Air Liaison Officers are stationed at Nyeri and Nakuru. Their duties are:—

    (i) To advise all ground force units in their area of the correct use of air support and assist in planning.

    (ii) To obtain intelligence information for the J.O.C.

    (iii) To ensure by constant liaison visits that the best use is made by the ground force of the air effort available.

Command and Control

5. The command and control of this force is exercised through the Joint Operations Centre (J.O.C.) at General Headquarters, Nairobi, to which all demands for offensive air support are sent either direct or through brigades.

Section 2—Types of Support

6. The types of air operations carried out under the jurisdiction of the J.O.C. fall into five broad categories:—

(*a*) Light Liaison Support.

(*b*) Offensive Support—

    (i) Immediate;

    (ii) Pre-planned.

(*c*) Transport Support—

    (i) Air Supply;

    (ii) Communications (Note 1);

    (iii) Casualty Evacuation (Note 2)

(*d*) Photographic Reconnaissance.

(*e*) Psychological Warfare.

Note 1.—The Tri Pacer aircraft based at Mweiga and Nakuru can be used only for operational purposes. Two communication aircraft are located at Nairobi West and are available for routine communication flying on application to (Mov.), General Headquarters.

Note 2.—This is carried out under the auspices of the Medical Branch (*See* Chapter XX).

Light Liaison Support

7. This is carried out by the Tri Pacers of the Kenya Police Reserve Air Wing, and comprises:—

(a) Contact Reconnaissance.
(b) Limited supply dropping.
(c) Operational Reconnaissance by day and night.
(d) Artillery Reconnaissance.

8. While the majority of these tasks are self explanatory, 7 (a) may require some clarification. There are two inherent difficulties connected with ground operations in the forest areas of Kenya. One is communications and the other accurate map reading during a prolonged patrol. All Tri Pacers are equipped with 88 sets and are therefore able to contact forest patrols direct. This provides an invaluable means of relaying messages and pin-pointing ground positions. This type of air support carried out by the Kenya Police Reserve Air Wing is known under the general term of "Contact Reconnaissance".

Offensive Support

9. Offensive support is normally called upon to achieve one or more of the following aims:—

(a) To destroy terrorist hides and to inflict casualties.
(b) To harass and lower morale.
(c) To drive terrorists out of an area which cannot easily be reached by ground forces.

Pre-planned Support

10. The main weight of the offensive effort is utilized on pre-planned support. This can be either in conjunction with, or completely divorced from, ground action. The planning of this type of support is carried out at the J.O.C. based mainly on photographic interpretation on a broad directive from the Commander-in-Chief. In order to give the Air Force the necessary freedom of action, it may be necessary for ground forces to vacate temporarily their forest operational areas. It should be borne in mind, however, that units and brigades may request a pre-planned air programme in support of their own operations to achieve one of the aims given in paragraph 9 above.

Immediate Support

11. This is requested by the ground forces and is for air action within 24 hours of the request being made. The weight of effort is allocated on the information passed by the requesting formation. Detailed information regarding the type of target, its location and position of own troops is required if the support is to be rapid and effective. The decision as to the weight of effort is made at the J.O.C. and is dependent upon this information.

12. At Appendix "A" is an Aide Memoire for demanding offensive support.

Mushroom Procedure

13. While normally aircraft are only used offensively within the prohibited areas, light aircraft (Pacers and Harvards), using 20-lb. bombs only, may be employed outside these areas in certain conditions:—

   (a) Air attack will only be undertaken at the request of the military commander on the ground when in close contact with a terrorist gang large enough to offer a reasonable target for air attack.

   (b) The military commander on the ground will only employ that degree of force which is necessary to achieve the object of his operations.

   (c) There will be no indiscriminate or independent bombing operations.

   (d) Air attack will only be undertaken when there is no foreseeable danger of injury to innocent persons.

   (e) Only specially selected pilots will be employed.

Requesting Procedure

14. When a terrorist gang is contacted outside the prohibited areas, the military commander will call initially for a Pacer contact reconnaissance aircraft. On arrival of the Pacer, ground to air communication will be established on the 88 set. A decision to take offensive air action will then be made as a result of consultation between the military commander and the pilot.

15. If the pilot is qualified, and the Pacer armed, action can be taken immediately. It may be necessary, however, for the Pacer to call additional aircraft.

16. Full details of the procedure to be used are contained in General Headquarter Operational Instruction No. 20 dated 3rd June, 1954, and J.O.C. Directive 4/54 dated 9th June, 1954.

Air Supply

17. The type of aircraft and the method to be used is dependent upon the scale of the ground operation. For reasons of economy and simplicity the maximum use is made of free dropping from Tri Pacer aircraft. The method of calling for supply by this means is contained in Section 4 of Chapter XIX.

18. When it is necessary to mount a ground offensive involving a major air supply the planning is carried out by the J.O.C. in conjunction with the brigade/brigades involved. This type of air supply is carried out normally by a Valetta aircraft, provided from Aden, parachuting S.E.A.C. Packs.

Photographic Reconnaissance

19. The photographic resources of the Command are limited. It is essential that the most economical use is made of all P.R. sorties and strict control is maintained at the J.O.C.

20. While a large proportion of the effort available is used for planning air attacks, some effort can be diverted for use by ground forces. Owing to the inaccuracy of the G.S.G.S. 1/50,000 series of maps, up-to-date photographic cover may be an essential preliminary to planning. Demands for photographic cover should be submitted to General Headquarters through the normal channels.

Psychological Warfare

21. Speech broadcasting and leaflet dropping is carried out by Auster aircraft over the prohibited areas. Co-ordination of this form of warfare is carried out by a joint committee under the chairmanship of a representative of the African Information Service.

22. Requests for speech broadcasting are submitted by units through brigades to the representative of the African Information Service in their area who will in turn submit it through their Director to the J.O.C.

Section 3—Methods of Calling for Air Support
Light Liaison Support

23. Requests for all types of light liaison support are normally submitted by units through battalions and brigades to the G.L.O. at Mweiga.

24. Patrols in the forest requiring additional support are at liberty to arrange such support direct with the Pacer pilot on the 88 set since this may often be their only means of communicating with Headquarters outside the forest.

Offensive Support

25. Requests for offensive air support are normally passed to the J.O.C. through battalions and brigade. There are, however, two exceptions—
 (a) Under the Mushroom procedure laid down in paragraph 13 above.
 (b) Requests for immediate support by patrols whose only means of contact is through the Pacer aircraft.

26. A diagram showing the detailed methods of calling for light liaison and offensive support is at Appendix "B" to this chapter.

APPENDIX "A" TO CHAPTER XIV
AIDE-MEMOIRE FOR DEMANDING AIR SUPPORT

Detail	Remarks
A.—TASK:	
(i) Fmn or Unit	
(ii) Map Ref of tgts	
....	
....	
....	

(iii) Background to Op and info on which based

  The better the info the bigger the air effort likely to be put on.

(iv) What strike is expected to achieve

  Type of a/c and armament depends on this.

B.—TIME AND DURATION:

(i) Time and date reqd on tgt ....

(ii) Duration of strike ....

(iii) Time after which no air action acceptable

(iv) Details of any acceptable postponement ....

  Alternative time if possible.

  } In case of bad weather.

C.—PSN OF OWN TPS:

(i) Map Refs or distance and direction from tgt

(ii) Intention of own tps after strike

D.—SPECIAL INSTRS:

(i) ....

(ii) ....

  Low flying over Reserve for morale purposes? Strafing?

APPENDIX "B" TO CHAPTER XIV
DIAGRAM SHOWING CHANNELS FOR CALLING FOR AIR SUPPORT

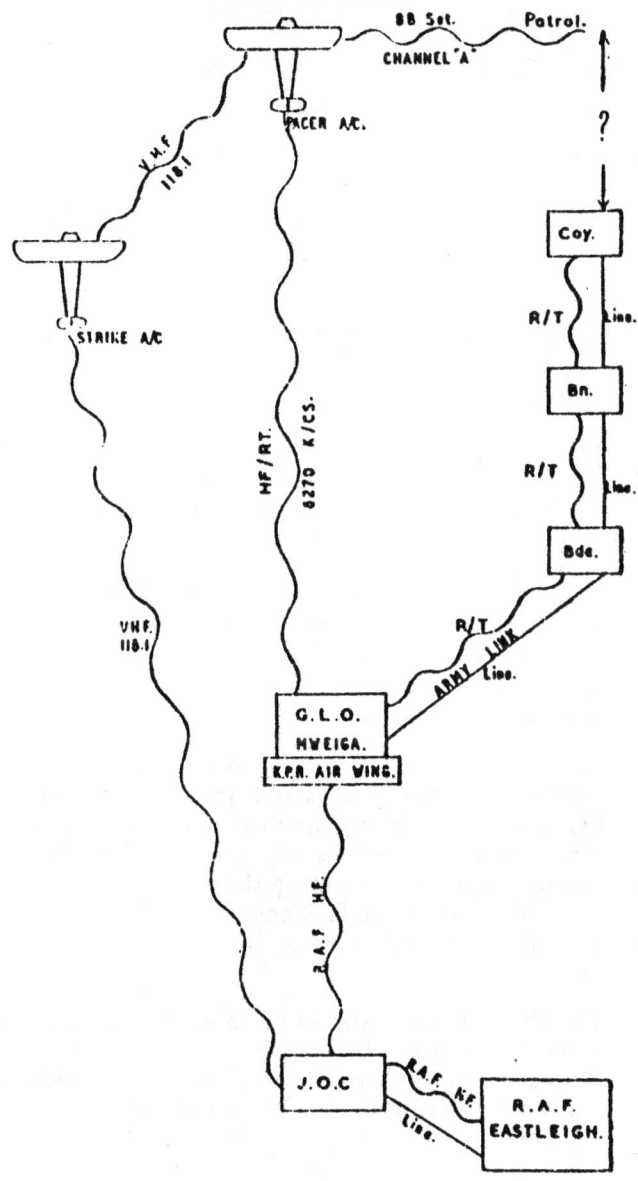

CHAPTER XV—TRAINING

Section 1—General

Training is considered under three main headings:—

(*a*) Training before arrival in East Africa.

(*b*) Initial training in East Africa.

(*c*) Training to maintain operational efficiency.

Section 2—Training Before Arrival in East Africa

Small Arms Training

1. The most important requirement in anti-Mau Mau operations is for every individual to be able to fire a quick, accurate shot, at comparatively short range at a moving target, from the standing or kneeling position.

2. The most effective way of training men up to this standard is to practise them firing at a No. 11 figure target at 30 yards' range from both kneeling and standing positions. When the men can hit their targets confidently from a stationary position, they should walk up the range from the 100-yard firing point and open fire on the appearance of targets which appear at irregular intervals. Men should be trained to get two shots off at each exposure at any range from 50 to 25 yards. Once the men can hit their targets under these conditions they should be practised in a similar manner but at the double.

3. The above range practices should be carried out with rifles, S.M.C.s and L.M.G.s. It is rare in forest operations for the L.M.G. numbers to have time to lie down and assume the normal firing position. L.M.G.s are normally fired from the hip, the weapon being supported by a sling, or from the shoulder. Firing from the shoulder requires greater physical strength, but if the men can be trained to do it, far more accurate fire can bee attained.

4. The above practices should be varied with snap practices from the standing and kneeling positions at figure targets which do not appear from exactly the same place and which move a yard or two to the left or right during each exposure.

Physical Fitness

5. Owing to the fact that they carry little, Mau Mau gangs travel very fast. Pursuits are often necessary at high speed over long distances. All troops should, therefore, before coming to East Africa, be brought to a high pitch of physical fitness, with cross-country running to augment marching.

Fieldcraft

6. It is unlikely that battalions coming to East Africa can be given practical instruction in the forest conditions encountered in the operational areas of Kenya. It is, however, felt that the officers should lecture their men, as soon as East Africa is known to be their destination, to acclimatize their minds to the standard of mental alertness which successful forest operations involve.

7. At the very outset men should be made to understand that they are going to be playing a game of blind man's buff with a very skilled adversary. He is constantly on the watch for visible signs of the security forces, who must never play into his hands by leaving such signs as a cigarette end, a path or bruised vegetation indicating where they have left the main track, or a trail of snapped twigs which some thoughtless member of a patrol has plucked off trees as he passes.

8. Troops must themselves use all the tricks of fieldcraft practised by the Mau Mau and described in Section 4 of Chapter VI. As time has gone on the Mau Mau have introduced more and more tricks to improve their fieldcraft. There is endless scope for British junior leaders likewise to think up new ways of deceiving the enemy.

9. Another matter which should be impressed early on the men is the need for absolute silence in the forest. The Mau Mau are constantly listening as well as watching for signs of the security forces. From the moment a patrol enters the forest until the time its operation is concluded no word should be spoken aloud except for fire orders, etc., after contact with the enemy has been made. There are, of course, exceptions, i.e. when in close proximity to fast-running mountain streams which drown the noise of speech, but until the standard of fieldcraft becomes such that exceptions are self-evident, silence must be the rule.

10. To assist silent movement, rubber-soled jungle boots are worn on forest operations, but lack of skill in avoiding dead twigs, failure to muffle the rattle of some piece of equipment or an inability to control a tickling throat can paint an accurate picture of a patrol's progress to a listening enemy.

11. Finally it should be put to the men that the application of good fieldcraft will result in successful contacts with the enemy and the feeling of a good job well done. The alternative is hour after hour of futile patrolling, with no action to relieve tedium or tiredness, and a return to base with a feeling of frustrated failure.

Specialist Training

12. The only specialists who are required in greater numbers than in other theatres are signallers. Twenty-five per cent extra signallers should accordingly be trained before arrival in East Africa. Notes on the types of sets used and advice on erecting the various forms of aerials which have been found effective under local conditions are given in detail in Chapter XVII.

Section 3—Initial Training in East Africa

Advance Parties

13. Operations/Training advance parties normally precede new battalions posted to East Africa. These advance parties are briefed on operational requirements, carry out attachments to units located in the areas in which their battalions will be deployed and attend courses at the East Africa Battle School. At this school fieldcraft, jungle tactics and the correct use of native trackers and war dogs are taught.

14. On the arrival of the main body these advance parties are available to assist in the training of the men of their battalions whilst a proportion of the officers attend courses at the Battle School.

Main Bodies

15. Four weeks' acclimatization is required before any individual may take part in operations. This is made necessary by the height and climate. During this period training will take the following lines:—

    (a) *Company and Platoon Commanders* will attend a course at the Command Battle School.

(b) The rest of the battalion will carry out training under the members of the advance party. Such training will include fitness training (such as route marches including periods of doubling), jungle range, patrols and ambushes.

(c) Every effort will be made to obtain a working knowledge of Swahili since all ranks will find this useful for intercourse with native trackers, guides, African members of the Armed Forces, Police and the African civilian labour which is allocated to all British battalions. Swahili is a very simple language to learn and is picked up by the average askari, who has probably spoken nothing but his own tribal language until joining the Army, in about two to three months. A book recommended is "Up-country Swahili" by S. H. Le Breton, price 3/6d., Publishers R. W. Simpson & Co., Ltd., Richmond, Surrey. A list of useful Swahili words is attached as Appendix "A" to this Chapter.

Section 4—Training to Maintain Operational Efficiency

16. It is not proposed to lay down in this handbook the exact form that training to maintain operational efficiency must take. The following points must, however, be borne in mind by commanders at all levels.

17. **Fitness.**—Men who have had a spell away from operations, i.e. signallers at battalion headquarters, regimental police, men who have been sick—all require physical fitness training before they are competent to undertake the rigours of operational patrolling at high altitudes.

18. **Marksmanship.**—Since contacts are comparatively rare to the individual soldier, his shooting must be kept up to a high standard by constant practice between operations. To simplify the accounting, ammunition expended on training in the operational area is classified as fired operationally. It follows that every company should construct a jungle range whenever it moves to a new location and however short its stay is likely to be. With practice a jungle range can be constructed in two to four hours. Notes on construction are at Appendix "B" to this Chapter.

19. **Fieldcraft.**—New tricks and signs employed by the Mau Mau are constantly being discovered. These are taught at the Battle School and in this way passed on to battalions, which should encourage periodic discussions of patrol commanders to pool such information.

20. **Signal Training.**—New techniques for improving wireless communication in the forest are produced at intervals. These must be studied and practised by unit signallers.

21. **General.**—The normal training to maintain such specialists as drivers, etc., is self-evident and requires no special mention.

22. **Summary.**—The enemy in Kenya is constantly improving his fieldcraft as he knows that his survival depends upon it. Troops deployed against the Mau Mau must never therefore be allowed to feel that they have reached perfection.

APPENDIX "A" TO CHAPTER XV
LIST OF SWAHILI WORDS

1. Figures

1	MOJA	20	ISHIRINI
2	MBILI	30	THELATHINI
3	TATU	40	AROBAINI
4	NNE	50	HAMSINI
5	TANO	60	SITINI
6	SITA	70	SABINI
7	SABA	80	THEMANINI
8	NANE	90	TISINI
9	TISA	100	MIA MOJA
10	KUMI	200	MIA MBILI
11	KUMI NA MOJA	250	MIA MBILI NA HAMSINI
12	KUMI NA MBILI, etc.		

2. Words Denoting Time

(a) Sunday JUMA PILI
    Monday JUMA TATU
    Tuesday JUMA NNE
    Wednesday JUMA TANO
    Thursday ALHAMISI
    Friday JUMAA
    Saturday JUMAMOSI

(b) *Hours*
    Hour SAA
    Clock, watch SAA
    Week WEEKI (or WIKI)
    Year MWAKA
    Daytime MCHANA
    Night USIKU

The time is told from sunrise and from sunset in 12 hours periods i.e. 0700 hrs. is reckoned as 1 o'clock, or in Swahili--saa moja. Midnight and midday are both half-way through the 12-hour period and are therefore 6 o'clock or saa sita.

3. Useful Phrases and Words

How many?	NGAPI?
How old?	NI YA SASA AU YA ZAMANI?
Loaded	WANA MIZIGO
Unloaded	BILA MIZIGO
Food carriers	WATU WA KUCHUKUA CHAKULA
Fresh	YA SASA HIVI
Old	YA ZAMANI
Go right	KWENDA KUSHOTO
Go left	KWENDA KULIA
Stop/halt/stand up/stand still	SIMAMA
Come back	RUDI
Carry on	ENDELEA
Go straight on	KWENDA MBELE
Hideout	KAMPI YA MAU MAU
Woman	BIBI
Children	WATOTO
Rifle	BUNDUKI
Gang	KUNDI
Food	CHAKULA
Work	KAZI
People	WATU
Road, track	NJIA (main road is BARABARA)
Soldier	ASKARI
Meat	NYAMA
Bamboo	MIANZI
Tree	MTI
In the forest	NDANI YA MSITU
In the bush (or scrub)	NDANI PORINI
and	NA
Cattle	NG'OMBE
Sheep	KONDOO

Goat	MBUZI
Here	HAPA
There	PALE (KULE)
Behind	NYUMA
Beyond	
In front	MBELE
Before	
Quickly	UPESI
Slowly	POLE POLE
With	NA
Narrow	NYEMBAMBA
Wide	PANA
Long	MREFU
Short	MFUPI
Wait	NGOJA
Large	KUBWA
Small	DOGO
Above	JUU
Below	CHINI
Be quiet	NYAMAZA
Listen	SIKILIZA

4. Game Animals

Elephant	NDOVU	Leopard	CHUI
Rhino	KIFARU	Hyena	FISI
Buffalo	MBOGO	Monkey	NUGU or KIMA
Buck	NYAMA or FUNO or MNYAMA	Baboon	NYANI

5. Questions to a Prisoner

Q. Are you a food carrier   KAZI YAKO NI KU-CHUKUA CHAKULA KWA KUNDI?

A. Yes.   NDIO

Q. Where were you going?	ULIKUWA UNA KWENDA WAPI or UNAKWENDA WAPI?
A. We were going to (reserve/our camp)	TULITAKA KUFIKA (RESERVE/KAMPI YETU)
Q. How many were in your gang?	WATU WANGAPI WALIKUWA NDANI KUNDI YAKO?
A. (Here a number may be given)	
Q. Are any in possession of firearms in your gang?	WAKO WATU WA BUNDUKI NDANI KUNDI YAKO?
A. No.	HAPANA
Q. Where is your hideout?	WAPI KAMPI YAO?
A. I will show you	NITAWAONYESHA NINYI
Q. Have they any sentries to guard the road to their camp?	WANA ASKARI YA KUCHUNGA NJIA KWA KAMPI YAO?
A. I do not know	SIJUI
Q. Do you know this area?	WAJUA NCHI HII HAPA?
A. I know it well.	NAJUA SANA
Q. Is there a stream near?	IKO MTO KARIBU?
A. No. it is far away.	NI MBALI SANA
Q. What were they doing?	WALIKUWA WAKIFANYA NINI?
A. They were looking for food	WALIKUWA WANATAFUTA CHAKULA
Q. Is your camp far?	KAMPI YENU NI MBALI?
A. It is nearby.	NI KARIBU
Q. How far ahead are they?	KUNDI NI MBALI GANI MBELE?
A. They have dispersed	WAMETOROKA KABISA

6. **Questions to a Tracker**

Q. Have you seen (or found) signs of feet?	UMEONA ALAMA ZA MIGUU?

Q. Have you lost the tracks?	UMEPOTEA ALAMA ZA MIGUU?
Q. Why are you stopping?	KWA SABABU GANI UNASIMAMA?
Q. How many men were there?	WALIKUWAPO WATU WANGAPI?
Q. At what time did they pass here?	WAMEPITA HAPA SAA
A. One hour ago.	TANGU MUDA WA SAA MOJA
A. Twenty minutes ago.	DAKIKA ISHIRINI ZIMEPITA
Q. Did they disperse at this place?	WAMETAWANYA HAPA? or WAMETOROKA TOKA HAPA?
Follow one of the middle tracks.	FUATA NJIA MOJA KATIKATI WAMEPITIA
Tell me when you think we are getting near the enemy	NIAMBIE WAKATI UNATHANI TUNAKARIBIA KARIBU NA MAADUI
The enemy are near now	MAADUI (or WAGAIDI) NI KARIBU SASA
I will use a dog to smell the track (along which they passed)	NITATUMIA MBWA KUNUSA NJIA (WALIYOPITIA)

APPENDIX "B" TO CHAPTER XV

NOTES ON CONSTRUCTION OF A JUNGLE RANGE

General

1. A jungle range is no more than a winding path or track through a small area of forest around which targets have been prepared which can be moved into the view of a man walking down the track. In certain positions, for instance just round a sharp bend in the track, a stationary target is sufficient to force the man to take a quick snapshot.

2. Troops requiring practice at jungle shooting walk down the track one at a time and engage the targets which are made either to swing out at them from behind trees or to spring upwards from behind low cover.

Hints on Simple Target Mechanisms

3. **The Swinging-out Target.**—The most simple method of making a target swing out from behind a tree is to screw the target to the tree using old door hinges. The target can be held back in a position, obscured from the firer by the tree trunk, by an old spring or piece of elastic. The target operator can then swing the target into view by pulling a piece of string or wire attached to the outer side of the target.

4. **The Spring-up Target.**—There are two simple methods of making a target spring up vertically from a position flat on the ground. Each method requires the target to be joined, by simple hinges, to a rough wooden base board:—

(a) The target is held back by a piece of elastic or a weak spring and pulled up by wire or string in a similar manner to the swing-out target.

(b) The tension of the spring or elastic is at the front so that the normal position of the target is upright. When prepared for a surprise appearance the target is forced back against the pressure of the spring and a stone or other weight placed on it which is attached to a string or wire. A pull on the latter will remove the weight and cause the target to spring upright.

5. **The Crossing Target.**—This type of target can be simply made by fixing a taut wire at a fairly steep angle between two trees astride the track. The target can either be suspended from the wire by a small pulley wheel or, if the latter is not available, the wire can be greased and a simple hook, attached to the top of the target, made to fit over it. The target is held in position at the higher end of the taut wire and when released will travel along it and across the track, at a speed which is dictated by the angle of the taut wire. If part of the track is selected where there is narrow visibility the appearance of this type of crossing target can be effective and unexpected.

Work Required

6. It will be seen from the foregoing that once a sub-unit has provided itself with some hinges, springs or elastic, wire and odd pieces of wood, it can quickly prepare semi-permanent gadgets which can be adapted to any piece of forest in a very short time. Once the basic target mechanisms have been constructed they can be moved from tree to tree or cover to cover so that variety can be obtained each time the range is used.

7. A suitable track may well be already available but if not, a lane can be very quickly cut since it does not matter how much it twists and so the easiest path can be taken.

Safety Precautions

8. The safest location in which to site a jungle range is in a narrow valley with higher ground to the front and sides. If the company or platoon base is in or near a settled area particular care is necessary to see that overs and ricochets will not endanger the community. When in doubt the local representative of the Administration should be consulted.

9. The safety arrangements for the operators of the targets must be planned with extreme care. Some of these must inevitably be in front of the start point of the track in order that they can ensure that their targets come up at the right time in relation to the position of the firer. The officer laying

out the range must therefore keep a "bird's eye" view of the layout in his mind since, owing to the twisting of the track or firing lane, and the fact that the undergrowth may be thick, the operator of any one target is most unlikely to be visible from the preceding firing point. Target operators who come within the arc of fire of any firing point must be in pits or protected by some natural feature giving cover from fire.

10. Care must be taken that the last man is back behind the start point before the next man goes down the lane. It is best to have two groups here so that men who have fired cannot tell the others what surprises are in store.

CHAPTER XVI
FIELD ENGINEERING
Section 1—Introduction
Aim
1. The aim of this Chapter is two-fold:—
   (a) To give reference to the relevant manuals and pamphlets on subjects which are contained therein.
   (b) To give instruction in practices and techniques which have been evolved in the current operations in Kenya.

2. The most important bugbear with which field engineers of all arms have to contend in Kenya is rain; heat is also a factor. However, in principle field engineering in Kenya does not differ from field engineering elsewhere.

Abbreviations
3. The following abbreviations are used in this Chapter:—

In Full	Abbreviation
Field Engineering and Mine Warfare Pamphlet No. 1, Basic Field Engineering, Part I—All Arms, 1950, W.O. Code No. 8503	F.E.M.W. 1, Pt. I
Field Engineering and Mine Warfare Pamphlet No. 2, Field Defences and Obstacles, Part I—All Arms, 1951, W.O. Code No. 8666	F.E.M.W. 2, Pt. I
Field Engineering and Mine Warfare Pamphlet No. 3, Demolitions, Part I—All Arms, 1953, W.O. Code No. 8776	F.E.M.W. 3, Pt. I
Field Engineering and Mine Warfare Pamphlet No. 7, Booby Traps, 1952, W.O. Code No. 8741	F.E.M.W. 7
Public Works Department	P.W.D.

Section 2—Fieldworks
Slit Trenches
4. Two-men slit trenches are generally considered necessary on the perimeter of all camps which are likely to be occupied for more than a week. They should be six feet long, two feet six inches wide and four feet six inches deep with a sump at

one end. No precautions need be taken about camouflage or disposal of the soil, which should be disposed of on the up-hill side to prevent water flowing into the trench.

5. The sump can conveniently be the size of a four-gallon non-returnable tin. A tin is then let into the sump and when it is full of water it can be easily removed and emptied. This method of emptying the sump is more convenient than the normal one of baling.

6. No splinter-proof overhead cover is required. As a protection against sun and rain a simple cover can be made consisting of four posts and a grass or leaf thatch. This cover must overlap the trench and allow rain to fall away on the down-hill side.

Wiring

7. The most economical fence to build in terms of labour and stores is the single catwire fence. Details of this and other fences are given in F.E.M.W. 2, Pt. I, Section 59 and Appendices "L" to "P".

Section 3—Clearing Trees and Bamboo

Trees

8. Saplings and trees up to about four inches in diameter can best be cleared with hand tools. Larger trees, however, take a long time to clear by hand and explosives are therefore quicker and easier. Tables showing times, quantities of explosives and labour required for felling trees are given in Section 4 to this Chapter.

9. When bulldozers are available they can be used for felling trees up to about eighteen inches in diameter. For larger trees explosives are more economical. It is, of course, wasteful to move a bulldozer a long way to clear only a few trees.

Bamboo

10. No satisfactory method has yet been discovered of clearing bamboo by the use of explosives. Hand clearing must be used.

Section 4—Use of Explosives

11. F.E.M.W. 3, Pt. I, gives details of the service explosives and accessories in current use, how charges are prepared for firing, and safety precautions.

Tree-felling by Explosives

12. The Tables 1 and 2 below are shown quantities of explosives and labour constants for tree-felling. The best results are not obtained until the operators have gained experience with the actual types of tree concerned and their characteristics, weaknesses and root formation.

13. Felling by borehole charges uses only about half the quantity of explosive but takes a little longer. A further disadvantage is that a "shaving brush" stump is left in the ground. Where this does not matter and economy of explosive is a factor, this method is recommended.

14. Many trees have a natural lean and directional felling is then not easy. An experienced team can, however, usually put the tree in the required direction seven times out of ten.

15. It is usual to blow five to seven trees at once; the charges are connected in a ring main by detonating fuse. Safety fuse is normally used to initiate the ring main.

TABLE 1.—CHARGES PLACED IN HOLES 6 TO 9 INCHES DEEP BETWEEN ROOT BUTTRESSES

Diam. of tree taken at 3 ft. above ground	Average No. of charges per tree	Explosives required lb.			Working Party		Time Mins.
		852	808	GC	Soldiers	African Labour	
(a)	(b)	(c)	(d)	(e)	(f)	(g)	(h)
1	2	4	5	5	2	2	5
1½	2	6	7	7	2	2	5
2	3	8	10	10	2	2	8
2½	3	12	14	14	2	2	8
3	4	16	18	18	2	2	10
3½	4	18	20	22	2	2	10
4	4	20	24	28	2	2	10

NOTES

(a) For connecting the charges in each tree and for connecting neighbouring trees by ring main, allow 1 ft. cordtex per 1 lb. explosive.
(b) For firing by safety fuse, allow one detonator per 10 lb. of explosive and 1 ft. of safety fuse per 10 lb. of explosive.
(c) The African labour is used to dig the holes between the roots, using a panga or machet and for carrying explosives, etc. If no African labour is available four soldiers will be required.
(d) The charge indicated is the minimum to fell the tree clean and leave root and stump completely shattered.

TABLE 2.—CHARGES PLACED IN BOREHOLES IN TRUNK OF TREE

Diam. of tree taken at 3 ft. above ground	Explosive Required		Holes bored by hand Working party		Time Mins.	Holes bored mechanically Working party		Time Mins.
			Sappers	African Labour		Sappers	African Labour	
(a)	(b)	(c)	(d)	(e)	(f)	(g)	(h)	(j)
1	2	3	1	2	10	2	2	5
1½	2½	3½	1	2	10	2	2	5
2	4	5	1	2	10	2	2	5
2½	6	7	1	2	15	2	2	7
3	8	10	1	2	15	2	2	7
3½	10	12	1	2	20	2	2	10
4	12	15	1	2	20	2	2	10

NOTES
  (a) Scale of accessories as for Table 1.
  (b) African labour is used for hand auger boring, carrying, etc. If not available soldiers have to be used in lieu.
  (c) When holes are bored with compressor-driven auger, the native (or other unskilled labour) is required for man-handling the compressor trailer and air pipes.

16. If there is a shortage of explosive and there are no wood augers, or if only gun-cotton is available, trees can be felled by making a "V" cut in the trunk to a depth of one-quarter of the diameter of the trunk. The "V" cut is packed with explosive. The quantity of explosive required in pounds is three times the cube of the diameter in feet.

Breaking Rocks or Boulders

17. Rocks and boulders can usually be split by firing a charge placed on top. It is not possible to define the quantity of explosive required. The best method is to fire one pound first, and, if this is not enough, to increase the charge by a pound at a time until the rock is split. Nearly all rock found in the operational part of Kenya is soft.

Section 5—Mine Detectors

18. Mine detectors can be of great assistance in searching for arms and ammunition. The detectors must be properly tuned and the operators must be trained and experienced in using them.

19. Mine detectors are a mixed blessing when searching ground because they will pick up any metallic object. They will, however, save a lot of time when searching people and are also of great assistance when searching huts, particularly the roofs of huts.

Section 6—Booby Traps

20. Booby traps are of doubtful value in the current operations because of the danger of their being set off by our own forces or by game. Troops from other units can easily wander into the wrong area. An additional hazard is bombing, which may render the firing device so sensitive that it would be dangerous to make safe.

21. Should orders be given for booby traps to be laid, however, common devices for setting them are given in F.E.M.W. 7.

Section 7—Roads and Tracks

General

22. Road construction for operational purposes is limited to the construction of earth roads. These have two fundamental limitations:—

(*a*) They can be used in dry weather only.

(*b*) They need continuous maintenance.

23. For the purpose of this section a distinction will be made between roads and tracks. Roads should be capable of carrying normal military transport; tracks may vary between the roughest footpath and a jeepable track, and therefore usually require fuller definition.

24. Any form of road construction is a deliberate and lengthy affair, involving extensive reconnaissance, the movement of labour and heavy plant and the establishment of camps, as well as the normal maintenance of a detachment. In mountainous forest these factors are all accentuated, and the requirement for a road must be carefully considered, as it is very easy to dissipate effort on projects of limited value.

25. Tactical commanders should try and site their forest camps close to existing roads. The construction of a new road to a temporary position is for example, not an economical proposition.

26. Above all, the planning of road requirements must be carried out well in advance. It is not practicable to make sudden switches of construction effort to meet unforeseen needs. Reconnaissance, which may take several weeks cannot be hurried and construction cannot usefully begin until this reconnaissance is complete.

27. The estimate of work required must be made by experts. Estimates by amateurs are almost invariably inaccurate, "A few hours work for a bulldozer" may prove to be several weeks work for several items of plant. "Two days for a grader" has often turned out to be a job wholly impracticable for graders at all.

28. It is not possible to give an estimate of the rate of progress that can be expected because of the many factors involved. Of these factors the most important are the weather, the terrain, and the plant and labour available for the task. As a very rough guide a troop of a field squadron R.E. with additional plant can build three-quarters of a mile per week of new road through forest, in good weather. It makes little difference to the speed of work whether an old rough game track is being improved or a new alignment is being made.

29. The most important single requirement for road construction in Kenya is good drainage.

Construction and Maintenance

30. The basic principles of road construction and maintenance are given in F.E.M.W. 1, Part I, Chapter 4.

Section 8—Field Accommodation

31. F.E.M.W. 1, Part I, Section 25, gives details of the siting and layout of temporary camps. A few hints on improving the standard of comfort in tented camps are given below.

Drainage

32. The paramount importance of good drainage cannot be overstressed. Each tent or shelter needs a drain all round. Footpaths must be raised above the surrounding ground and must have a drain on each side.

Tents

33. The comfort in 180 lb. tents can be increased by raising them off the ground and therefore giving more headroom inside. A simple method of doing this is shown in Diagrams A and B.

34. The inside of a tent can be made cooler by raising the outer fly as shown in Diagram C.

Disposal of Waste Matter

35. The efficient disposal of waste matter in the field is of paramount importance in the prevention of fly-breeding and the control of intestinal diseases.

36. Urinals

(a) A simple type of funnel urinal can be made from two or three D.D.T. or biscuit tins, the top tin of which is perforated and sloped at an angle. The urinal is placed over a soakage pit about two feet square and two feet deep. This type of urinal is shown in Diagram D.

(b) When there are no tins a shallow trench must be dug as illustrated in Diagram E.

37. Latrines

(a) In semi-permanent camps the P.W.D. provide deep trench or bucket type latrines. Units are responsible for their maintenance.

(b) In temporary camps and bivouacs, units must dig shallow trench latrines. The trenches are dug in rows allowing five trenches for every hundred men. Each trench should be three feet long, one foot wide and two feet deep, with a space of at least two feet between trenches. A scoop or shovel must be provided for each man to cover his own deposit. The trenches must be filled in after twenty-four hours and the site marked.

38. Sullage Water

(a) All waste water must be passed through a grease trap. In semi-permanent camps grease traps are provided by the P.W.D. In temporary camps and bivouacs grease traps must be improvised.

(b) A design for an improvised grease trap is shown in Diagram F.

39. Disposal of Refuse

(a) Wherever possible all refuse must be burned. A design for an improvised incinerator is given in Diagram G.

(b) When it is not possible to burn refuse it must be buried in a deep pit, covered with at least eighteen inches of soil and well rammed.

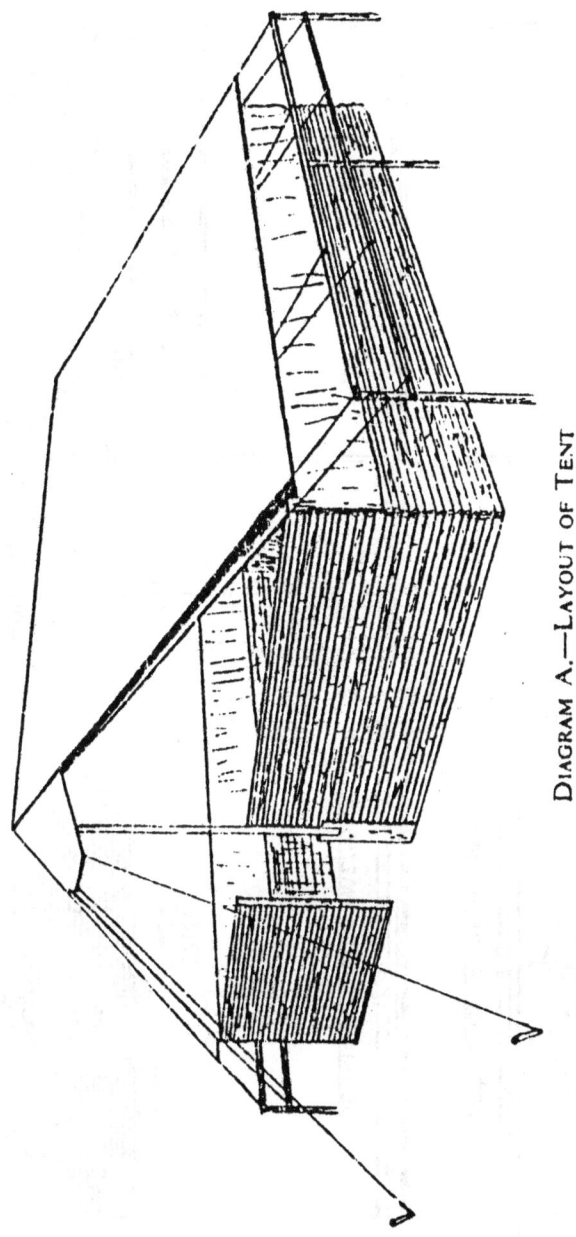

Diagram A.—Layout of Tent

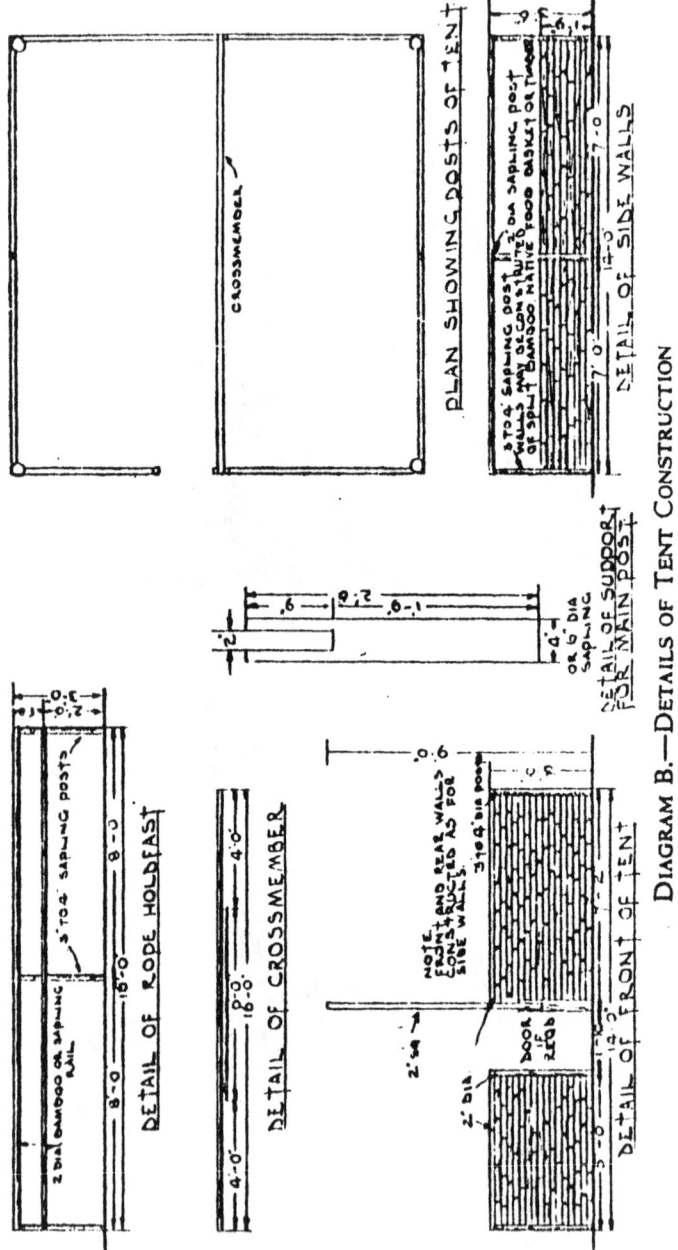

Diagram B.—Details of Tent Construction

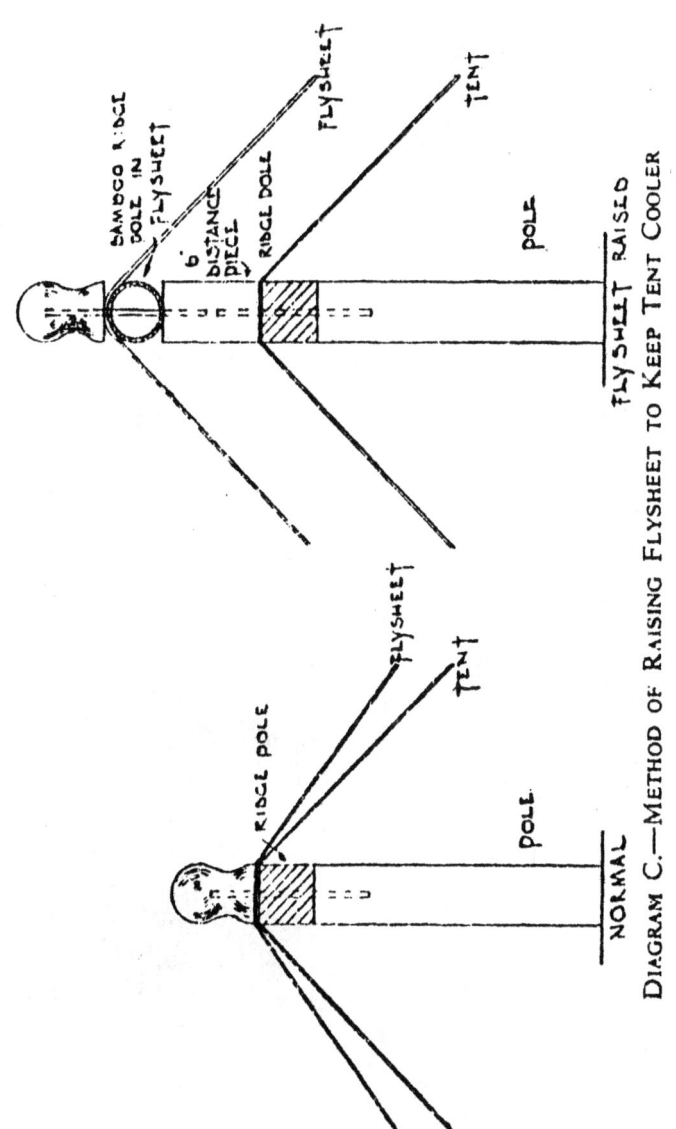

Diagram C.—Method of Raising Flysheet to Keep Tent Cooler

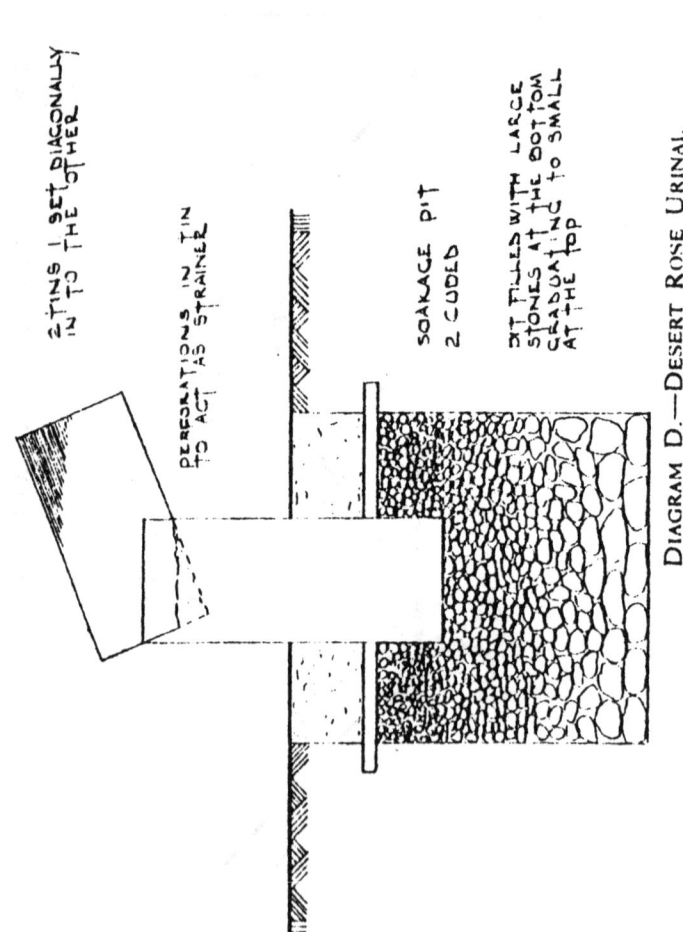

Diagram D.—Desert Rose Urinal.

DEPTH OF TRENCH - 6"
SOIL LOOSENED FOR A
FURTHER 6"
EXCAVATED EARTH
HEAPED ON THREE
SIDES - USED TO
RE-FILL WHEN CLOSED

DIAGRAM E.—SHALLOW TRENCH URINAL

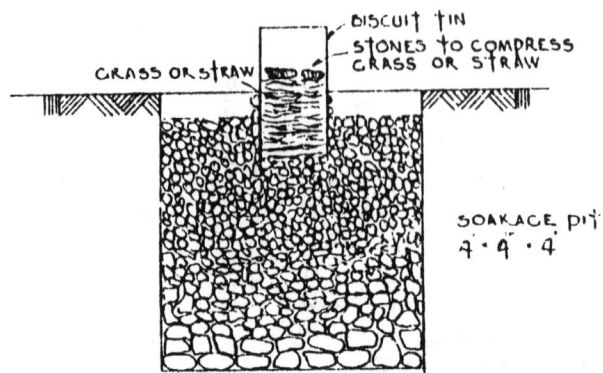

DIAGRAM F.—IMPROVISED GREASE TRAP

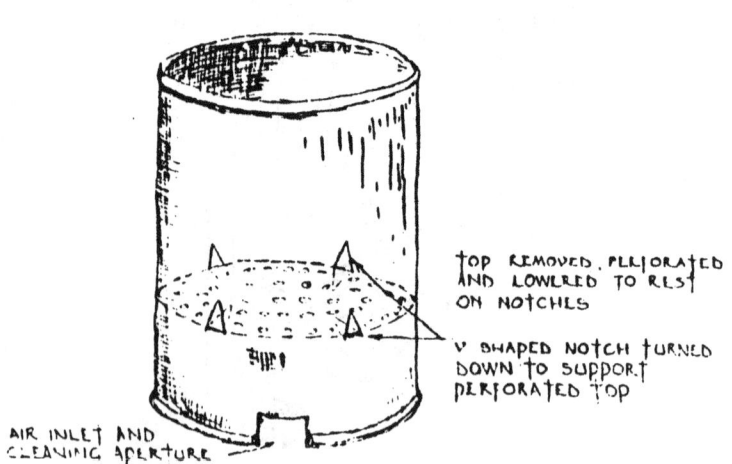

DIAGRAM G.—IMPROVISED OIL-DRUM INCINERATOR

CHAPTER XVII

SIGNAL COMMUNICATIONS

Section 1—General

1. Due to very considerable dispersion between and within units, signal communications in East Africa present special problems. Battalion Headquarters have on occasion been as much as 100 miles from their companies and companies up to 10 miles from their platoons. Even when more normal distances are the case, difficulties are experienced due to the screening effect caused by forests. Neither the Army nor the Posts and Telecommunications Department can meet all the line requirements of the security forces and wireless is therefore the backbone of the communication system.

2. Whenever possible line communication has been provided down to Battalion Headquarters, but care has to be taken not to whittle down the meagre line resources available to the Police and Civil Administration who are equally engaged in Emergency operations. Army line communication has been largely achieved by the extensive use of Army carrier equipment in order to superimpose circuits on existing civil routes. This equipment is handed over to the Posts and Telecommunications Department, who install, operate and maintain it in their own carrier rooms.

3. To ease the strain generally on both line and wireless communications a regular daily air despatch service is operated between General Headquarters and outlying military centres. This service has proved invaluable in saving time and wear and tear or vehicles. Deliveries of signals and letters by the air despatch service average around 18 hours from their time of origin and it is extremely important for all originators to frank their signals ADS when such a delay is acceptable.

Section 2—Types of Wireless Sets

4. Within the Infantry Battalion the following types of sets are used on a scaling shown below:—

W.S. 19/62/22 type	9
W.S. 46	20
W.S. 31	8
W.S. 88A	20
W.S. 88B	4

It will be noted that the scaling of H.F. sets has been increased at the expense of the V.H.F. sets (W.S. 31). This is in order to bridge the considerable distances between companies and platoons which the W.S. 31 could not span. More recently, improved aerial techniques, which will be discussed later, have greatly increased the normal range of both the W.S. 31 and 88.

5. Brigade and Command Signals are equipped with W.S. 19 and 53. A few W.S. 76 are also in use for static C.W. links and have proved quite satisfactory.

6. Mention should be made of the Police wireless communications which are both extensive and efficient. They operate in the order of 1,000 sets, of which practically all are in the V.H.F. band (80 megacycles). These are modern civilian pattern Marconi and Pye sets ranging from a manpack ($\frac{1}{4}$-watt) to vehicle and table sets (5 to 10-watts). In a country which lends itself to V.H.F. operation, the Police have obtained extremely effective results by careful siting of Police posts and the interchange of information over their V.H.F. network is both reliable and speedy.

Section 3—Wireless Nets

7. The standard Army nets are normally adhered to but in certain forest operations, when units are more concentrated, it is often found expedient for the whole battalion to work on one frequency—either an H.F. frequency using W.S. 19, 22, 62 and 46 or a V.H.F. channel using W.S. 31 and 88. This arrangement is very effective as all concerned from Battalion Headquarters down to patrol level can hear what is going on and should any one set be unable to contact another, several of the many sets on the net can, as a rule, act as relays. When operating on a single V.H.F. net, it is particularly effective if the light aircraft, in support of the unit is on the same frequency, so that it can act as a relay if required and also, with so many sets on its own frequency, it can be sure of making a contact with some part of the unit at any time it wishes to call up.

8. Police nets are mainly static operating, on a divisional basis. For example, all Police posts in the South Nyeri division are on the same frequency and are able to contact control direct. There are usually from 10 to 20 sets on any one net and, to avoid congestion, standard times during the hour are allotted

for different stations to make normal calls, although in an emergency any station can call up immediately. In addition to the static Police posts, there are generally four wireless-equipped patrol vehicles and four manpack sets in any one division for mobile contacts.

9. A considerable number of Police-type sets are held by Army units to enable them to work straight into the local Police net. These are very useful for tying in the Army with Police on operations or for maintaining contact with Army patrols operating in certain forest areas where Police V.H.F. sets have been found more effective.

Section 4—Overcoming Local Difficulties

10. Dispersion was the first difficulty to be overcome and this was solved by the use of H.F. skywave working, at which all units are now extremely proficient. By using this method Regimental Signal Officers need not be daunted by a requirement for R.T. for distances of 60 miles with a W.S. 62. H.F. suffers in East Africa from heavy static interference with the onset of darkness however; and this often blots out R.T. for several hours. K.A.R. battalions have managed to overcome this awkward period by using C.W. or M.C.W. signalling, as all African signallers are trained in morse. In an effort to find a solution to this difficulty a War Office team visited Kenya to investigate the use of more efficient aerials, particularly for V.H.F. sets. They evolved several aerials for W.S. 31 and 88, which boosted their range up to as much as 30 or 40 miles under good conditions. V.H.F. has now replaced H.F. for certain links within units and the night interference problem has been considerably decreased.

11. The final problem to be overcome is the organization of effective communication in the forest belts on the Aberdare range and Mount Kenya. Fortunately, these forests are on mountain slopes and consist of ridges and valleys so that it is possible to operate both H.F. and V.H.F. manpack sets in these areas, provided efficient aerials are used. In the case of V.H.F. working, an excellent solution is to site a W.S. 31 on a prominent feature at the foot of the forest belt which can look into the whole of a unit's operational area. This 31 set then acts as a

very effective relay for sets operating in the area. In addition, the use of aircraft flying overhead equipped with a W.S. 88 can be invaluable as a relay from patrols in thick forest to a firm base such as Company or Battalion Headquarters.

Section 5—Aerials

12. The two factors which decide the type of aerials which can be used are:—

(a) Those required for use in a static base.

(b) Those which are to be used in a mobile or manpack role.

These two factors are again subdivided into the type of set used, i.e. H.F. or V.H.F.

13. **H.F. Static Aerials.**—For brigade-battalion, and battalion-company communication the "SHIRLEY" aerial (described in Appendix "A") has proved to be the most efficient. Briefly it consists of two horizontally opposed half-wave folded dipole aerials erected between four poles of approximately 30–40 feet high. Its function is to concentrate the radiated power in an upward direction and thus it transmits and receives much more efficiently than a single wire over short and medium distances. Its construction is quite simple and well within the scope of unit production. It is essentially for use at a static base requiring a fairly flat area for its erection.

14. **H.F. Mobile Aerials.—**

(a) The distances involved and the forest conditions in which patrols operate preclude the use of H.F. ground-wave working. A simple sky-wave aerial is therefore essential.

(b) The 100-feet all-purpose aerial has proved to be the most simple and efficient for patrol use. No calculations are necessary in arriving at the correct length of wire for a specific frequency and its length represents about the longest acceptable in forest and difficult country.

(c) Another aerial which has produced excellent results is a half-wave folded dipole, details of which are given at Appendix "B". This aerial is a little more complicated in design and requires a greater length of wire than the

100-feet all-purpose aerial. It is, however, comparatively simple in construction and its erection produces no difficulties. Good results have even been obtained by two men holding up the aerial between them.

(d) The set/aerial combinations normally used in the battalion are:

Battalion and company base—W.S. 19/22/62—"SHIRLEY" aerial or 3/4 wave end fed.

Platoon/patrol—W.S. 46—100-ft. all-purpose aerial.

15. V.H.F. Static Aerials.—A very considerable improvement in signal strength to and from the W.S. 31 has been obtained by the use of an elevated half-wave aerial with reflecting plane—locally known as the "NANYUKI Mk. I", details of this aerial are contained in Appendix 'C'. This aerial consists of a 12-feet rod mounted on a 30/40-feet pole; the top sections of the guys supporting the pole are each made from 12 feet of stranded copper wire which provide the reflecting plane. The radiating element of the aerial is fed from the set by means of a coaxial or low loss cable. Ranges of 30 to 40 miles have been obtained between static stations suitably sited. This aerial is more suited for use at a static location such as battalion or company base but it is easily transportable (less pole), does not take up much ground space when erected and can and has been used successfully at a platoon base from which patrols operate.

16. V.H.F. Mobile Aerials.——

(a) Due to its weight and simplicity of operation the W.S. 88 has been much favoured for patrol work. Its normal 4-foot rod aerial, however, does not operate successfully in forest. Very good results have been obtained by the use of some 30 feet of copper wire, preferably insulated, slung over a tree and hauled into a vertical position. The combination of this form of elevated aerial working to a W.S. 31 and "NANYUKI Mk. I" aerial has given greater communication range to patrols.

(b) For the W.S. 31, vehicle mounted, a special type of aerial known locally as the "NANYUKI Mk. II" (details in Appendix "C") has been produced which gives a greater range to these sets when the vehicle is stationary. Briefly the aerial consists of a rotatable arm, mounted on the side of the vehicle, and upon which is mounted a radiating whip aerial (11 feet approximately) and a reflector rod. The aerial possesses distinct directional qualities at the longer ranges; the aerial is rotated to point at the distant station. Ranges of up to 35 miles have been obtained with the vehicle aerial workng to a "NANYUKI Mk. I".

17. In making all units "aerial conscious" particular stress has been and is being continually laid on the siting of sets and also the maintenance of equipment in good operating order as these two conditions are essential factors in the improved aerial techniques being practised in Kenya.

Section 6—Conclusion

18. Signalling under the conditions of wide dispersion imposed by the emergency calls for ingenuity and determination on the part of the unit signal officer. The Army wireless equipment in use is not basically designed for the distances involved. This problem can only be overcome by the use of the most efficient aerials, a high standard of regimental signallers, equipment maintained in proper working order and careful attention to siting. The co-operation of the battalion and company commander is essential to this last condition. Commanders must therefore locate their Headquarters on suitable sites to ensure the maximum efficiency of their wireless communications.

APPENDIX "A" TO CHAPTER XVII

THE CONSTRUCTION OF THE SHIRLEY AERIAL

1. The construction of the "Shirley" aerial is illustrated in the accompanying diagrams. These diagrams should be examined closely, together with the stores, which are as follows:—

Masts aerial (20 feet or higher)	4
Stakes, 6 feet	2
Insulators chain, 1 link	6
Insulators chain, 2 links	4
Transmission line, 150 ohm (telecon K24)	as required
Cable assault single for guys and halyards	as required
Insulation tape, rolls	1

2. (a) Calculate the length of the dipoles as follows:—
  Length of dipole (feet) = $\dfrac{468}{\text{Frequency mc/s}}$

  (b) Calculate the distance between dipoles:—
  Distance between dipoles (feet = 492 × 13/10 × frequency (mcs) (i.e. 0.65 wavelength).

3. Alternatively for the 68 set read off dipole length and spacing from the following table:—

OPTIMUM ELEMENT LENGTHS AND SPACINGS FOR W.S. 68 FREQUENCIES

Frequency in megacycles	Radiating element length in feet	Spacing between elements length in feet
3.75	134	182
3.75	125	170
4	117	160
4.25	104	142
4.05	104	142
4.75	98.5	135
5	93.5	127
5.02	90	122

Aerials with these characteristics should operate well ± 500 kcs from the Optimum frequency.

4. Inspect the ground. Ideal siting is:—

(a) Level ground clear of obstructions.

(b) Operating position midway between the element centres.

(c) Transmission lines coming in direct and at right angles to the radiating elements.

5. The perfect site will be found rarely. The aerial will, however, work with reduced efficiency on uneven ground and with obstructions such as wooden buildings and trees between the elements. The set need not be placed midway between the elements, but if it is not the transmission lines to the elements must be of equal length. Increasing the transmission lines from

50 feet to 100 feet each causes a reduction in power of only 0.4 dbs. Less than 100 feet should be sufficient for the majority of installations.

6. Cut the cable for the radiating elements, allowing two feet excess length for joints. Mark out the ground, using a compass to position the masts so that the aerials will be parallel and at right angles to a line joining their centres.

7. Attach insulator chain links to masts and weave cable assault through the links to act as halyards. Erect masts, using cable assault or other suitable materials as guys. Space the masts with allowance for halyards.

8. Fold the radiating elements in two and having located the centre mark it with string or tape. This is point B and B1 in Fig. 1.

9. Attach an insulator chain 2-link to each of the four halyards. Split each of the four ends of the two radiating elements for 3 inches, using a sharp blade. Strip the insulation off 1 inch of each of the twin wires thread through the appropriate insulator and bind the loop. Finally, join and insulate the conductors carefully as in Fig. 2. Each radiating element should now be strung on insulators in position between its masts but lying on the ground.

10. Cut each radiating element in the centre at point B and insert in each an insulator chain single link binding the loop of each cable with cord or tape as in Fig. 3. Ensure that about 4 inches of cable are left as a tail of each loop. Split each of the four tails with a sharp blade keeping the insulation intact Strip the insulation off 1 inch of each of the wires.

11. Take each element separately and carefully rejoint and insulate leads AB and BC at B, then A1 B1 and B1 C1 at B1. (*See* Figs. 1 and 3.)

12. Measure the distances of the cable route from the centre of the more distant element to the set. Cut two transmission lines to this length. It is essential that these lengths are made equal.

13. Split each of the four ends of the two transmission lines for 4 inches and strip the insulation off 1 inch of each of the

conductors. Loop and bind an end of one of these lines to each element centre insulator as in Fig. 3. Joint carefully and then insulate the conductors at D and E and then D1 and E1 as in Fig. B3.

14. Trace conductors DF and EG, then D1F and E1G right down each transmission line and label the set end. It is essential that no mistake is made.

15. Hoist each element. Drive in a 6-feet stake directly under the centre insulators of the elements and tape on the transmission line so that the strain is taken off the aerial. Ideally the set will be midway between the two element centres, but this will seldom be possible. Where it is not, run off the transmission line from the more remote element to the set keeping it close to the ground, and away from the radiating elements at as large an angle (ideally 90 degrees) as possible.

16. Run in the second transmission line to the set in the same way. Tie it back if necessary to take up the slack. On no account cut it as it must remain the same length as the other lines. Run the two transmission lines separately, looping them not closer than 3 inches apart.

17. At the set, join the two F Transmission line leads together and then two G leads. Connect one pair to the set earth terminal and the other pair to the set aerial terminal.

18. If the leads are mixed either at the join to the radiating elements or at the set the aerial will not work. It is not necessary to earth the set.

19. Tune the set in the ordinary way for maximum aerial current. Under most circumstances it will tune and load satisfactorily, but if it does not, connect to the aerial and earth terminals (in parallel with the transmission line leads) a 6-feet length of transmission line. The far ends of the conductors of this 6-feet lead should be open-circuited (i.e. separated and insulated). The cable may be coiled for convenience behind the set. It acts as a parallel capacity of 10.6 microfarads per foot.

20. Until the telecothene insulated K24 is available aerials may be made with plastic-covered twin copper lighting flex. The losses will be greater than with K24, but those tested have appeared very satisfactory, although the durability is not known. If such cable is purchased, it must be moisture-resistant and it

must be possible to trace the individual conductors either by colouring or observation. Insulated field cable with steel strands such as D8 should not be used to construct this aerial.

21. **Results.**—With the aerial used at one end of a link, signal strengths may be increased both on receive and transmit by the equivalent of a transmitter power increase up to three times compared with a dipole (depending on conditions); or by more than six times compared to an end-fed as usually installed. If the aerial is used at both ends of a link these power gains can be as high as 9 and 36 times respectively.

Fig. 1 of Appendix A.—Wiring Plan of Aerial

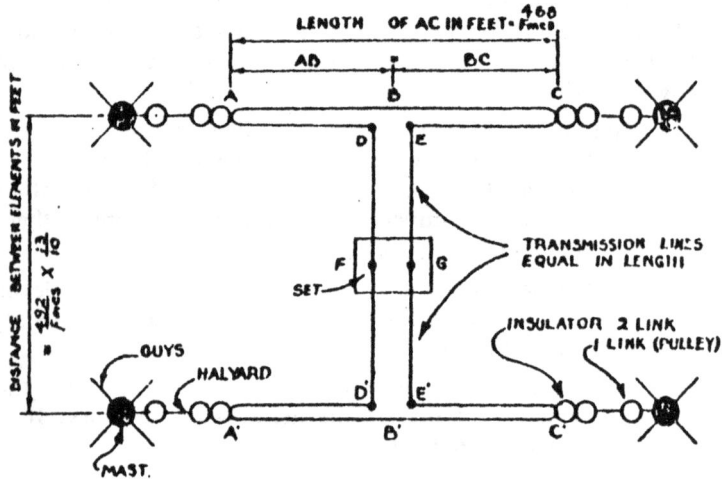

Fig. 2 of Appendix A.—Radiating Element

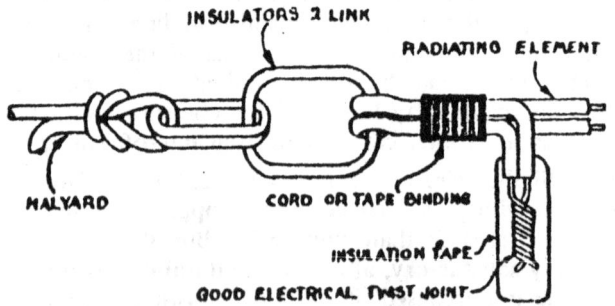

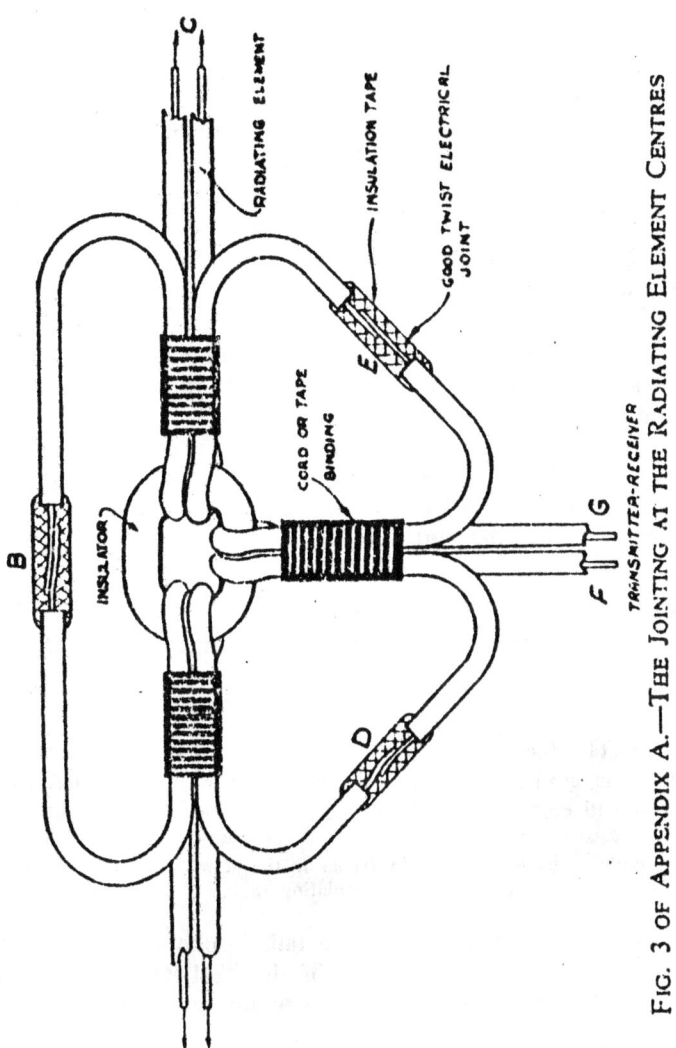

Fig. 3 of Appendix A.—The Jointing at the Radiating Element Centres

APPENDIX "B" TO CHAPTER XVII

HALF-WAVE FOLDED DIPOLE CONSTRUCTION

1. Formula for length of aerial:—

$$\frac{468}{\text{frequency (mc/s)}} = \text{Length in feet.}$$

e.g. 3.6 mc/s, length = 130 feet.

2. The wire to be used is flat twin lighting flex, not available in ORD but obtainable by local purchase.

3. Having cut the flex to the required length, insert at each end a shorting condenser of 500 pf value (these are very cheap items on local purchase).

4. At the exact centre point along the flex (e.g. 65 feet from one end at 3.65 mc/s), cut one leg of the twin wire flex, bare and splay the end thus:—

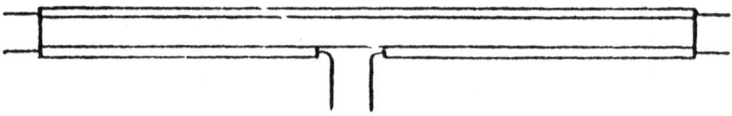

5. The feeder of the same twin flex cut to any convenient length is connected to the splayed ends and connected to the aerial and earth terminals of the set.

Note.—The jointing of the feeder to the aerial wire must be carefully carried out and protected with insulating tape.

6. The insertion of a single link insulator as described in the notes for the construction of the "SHIRLEY" aerial will greatly strengthen the centre point of the radiating wire.

7. The ends of the aerial should be attached to cords weighted at the ends to facilitate erection between two trees by the simple method of throwing the weighted cords over branches and hauling up to obtain maximum height.

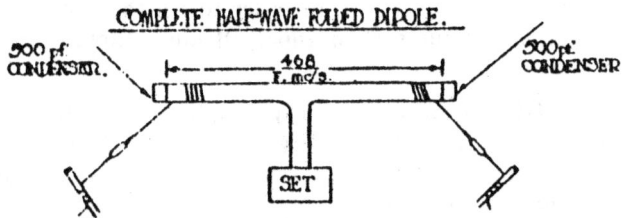

COMPLETE HALF-WAVE FOLDED DIPOLE.

This aerial is suitable not only for erection at a base but can also be taken out on patrol and erected between two trees or even held up in the air by two men each holding a bamboo pole or as a last resort holding the aerial themselves for quick temporary communications (note the loss of height in this case will cut down signal strength).

APPENDIX "C" TO CHAPTER XVII
Improved Aerials for the W.S. 31 and W.S. 88

1. The Army's V.H.F. sets, W.S. 31 and W.S. 88, have, for obvious reasons of weight and battery economy, only a very small power output. Their normal working ranges are therefore quite short. It is possible, however, markedly to improve the range obtainable by using more efficient aerial systems. It is the purpose of this note to describe two such aerials, one for use in static locations and the second a vehicle mounted aerial. Both aerials are developments in which standard practice is modified to suit the Army's special requirements.

2. In all communication systems employing V.H.F., the physical height of the aerial above the level of the surroundings is of the utmost importance. This point cannot be stressed too strongly and in using the aerials to be described, or, indeed, any VHF system, the first requirement is that, within the limits imposed by the tactical situation, the highest ground available should be used as the site of the station. This requirement applies equally to both ends of the link. For example, if a Command Post is controlling operations by means of V.H.F. sets, the Command Post should be sited on some prominent feature, and patrols should, wherever possible, report back from features such as ridges, etc., rather than from rivers and valley bottoms. Good siting at one end of the link will mitigate, to some extent,

shortcomings at the other, but in order to get the very best out of the communications system equal attention should be given to both ends.

The aerial developed for use in semi-static locations, such as brigade, battalion and company headquarters is an elevated half-wave rod mounted above a reflecting plane; the aerial for the vehicle on the move is a single half-wave whip which can be modified when the vehicle is stationary, by the addition of a single rod reflector. The reflector gives the aerial system an additional 4-5 dbs gain.

4. The construction and tuning of the aerials will now be described in detail.

The Elevated Half-wave Aerial with Reflecting Plane

5. **The Pole.**—The dimensions of the pole are not critical, but it should be as tall as possible. Thirty feet is a good height to aim at but if it can be made higher, so much the better. Until experiments can be done to assess the effects of metal poles, it is suggested that poles should be made of wood.

6. **The Radiating Element.**—The radiating element of the aerial is a 12 in. whip (F sections 1, 2, 3) mounted in a suitable aerial base (either No. 10 or No. 11 are suitable). The fixing of the base to the top of the pole depends upon the particular base used, and suggested methods are shown in figures 1 (A) and (B).

7. **The Reflecting Plane.**—The reflecting plane is present in "skeleton" form only, and is made from the top sections of the guy wires to the mast. The top sections of the guys are made from 12 ft. of copper wire with insulators at each end. These are fixed to the top of the mast as near as possible to the aerial base.

Not less than three wires should be used. More will give a closer approximation to a true reflecting plane, but three or four wires are quite sufficient. The copper wires are all joined together at the top by a linking copper wire which must not touch the mast. All the joints should preferably be soldered, but if this is not possible, good long wrapped joints should be made and they should be protected with insulating tape.

The remainder of the guy wires below the 12 ft. copper section can be made from rope or field cable. A point to be remembered is that the copper wire is not very strong, and during the erection of the mast too much stress should not be put on these guys. The bottom ends of the guys should be fixed in some convenient way and at such a distance from the base of the mast that the downward slope is not greater than about 45 degrees.

Figure 2 shows the construction of the reflecting plane.

8. **The Feeder.**—The aerial is fed via a twin-wire transmission line. The top end of the feeder is split, one wire going to the base of the 12 ft. whip and the second to the reflecting plane system. Again, the joints should be soldered if possible; if this is not possible, good electrical and mechanical joints should be made, and they should be covered with tape. The feeder line should be firmly anchored at the top of the mast with an insulated staple, to prevent the connections being subjected to mechanical stress. The feeder connections are shown in figure 3.

Any twin wire transmission line is suitable for use as the feeder. Telecon K.24 is a good low loss line, but if this is not available, the modern type of flat twin electric lighting flex can be used. Rubber insulated lines will introduce losses and should be avoided.

9. **Tuning the Aerial.**—The impedance between the feed point of the half-wave whip and the reflecting plane is high while the characteristic impedance of the twin wire feeder is low. Thus there is a mismatch at the aerial feed point which gives rise to standing waves of voltage and current along the line. The input impedance of the line varies along the line, being low at current loops and high at voltage loops. Both the W.S. 31 and the W.S. 88 output circuits are designed to work into high impedances and it is therefore necessary to cut the feeder to such a length that the set feeds into the correct high impedance.

There are two methods of adjusting the feeder to the correct length. In the first the actual r.f. current in the feeder is measured and in the second a modified W.S. 31 is used as a field-strength meter to measure the actual field strength produced by the aerial.

(a) R.F. Current Method

(1) Bring the feeder down from the aerial to the position which the set is finally to occupy, run off an extra ten feet, and cut.

(2) Somewhere between the desired final set position and the aerial, cut one wire of the feeder and insert a radio frequency milliameter, of range about 0-100 milliamps.

(3) Connect the two feeder wires to the aerial and earth terminals of the W.S. 31 or W.S. 88, and set to channel to be used.

(4) Switch set to send and read meter. Make note of reading.

(5) Cut off 6 in. of feeder. Reconnect to set making sure that same wires go to aerial and earth terminals.

(6) Switch set to send and read meter. Make note of reading.

(7) Repeat (5) and (6) until meter reading reaches a maximum value and begins to decrease.

(8) If the decrease below the maximum introduced by the final cut is not more than a few milliamps, the set can now be connected permanently to the feeder at this point. If a large decrease in feeder current was made by the final cut, replace the last few inches of feeder, tape the joins, and connect up to set.

(9) Remove meter and repair the cut in the feeder. (Figure 4 shows the set-up for tuning the feeder.)

NOTES

(1) It is possible by chance to cut the feeder for the meter at a point where the current is always nearly zero. If, after a few cuts have been taken off the end of the feeder, the current reading remains very small, take meter out and replace it about 3 ft. from original position.

(2) There may be a certain amount of unbalance in the system which gives rise to different currents in the two wires of the feeder. For this reason, during tuning, it is necessary to ensure that the same wires go to the aerial and earth terminals of the set.

(3) The position between maximum readings along the feeder is approximately 7 ft. 6 in. with Telecom K.24. If the first maximum found is at an inconvenient position for the set, it is possible to find another maximum about 7 ft. further up the feeder.

(4) The proximity of the feeder to ground can make an alteration in the meter current. During the tuning procedure keep the feeder, as far as possible, at a fixed distance above ground and from other objects.

(5) If the feeder is too large after tuning to come conveniently to the set position, do not coil the excess feeder, but loop it up in open curves.

(6) Switch the set off during adjustments to conserve the battery, so that consistent readings can be obtained.

(b) Field Strength Meter Method

(Details of the modification to the W.S. 31 which permits its use as a "field-strength meter" are given in Annexure 1.)

(1) Bring the feeder down from the aerial to the position which the set is finally to occupy, run off an extra 10 feet, and cut.

(2) Connect end of feeder to W.S. 31 or W.S. 88, switched to channel to be used.

(3) Place "field-strength meter" at a distance of a few hundred yards from aerial, transmit on W.S. 31 and note meter reading on "field-strength meter". It should be about mid-scale. Alter distance between aerial and "Field-strength meter" to bring reading to about mid-scale if required.

(4) Transmit on W.S. 31 and order "Read now". Keep carrier on for about ten seconds to enable "field-strength meter" operator to make reading.

(5) Listen on W.S. 31 while "field-strength meter" operator reports his reading, and make a note of reading.

(6) Cut 6 inches off feeder. Reconnect to set.

(7) Repeat 4, 5 and 6 until meter reading reaches a maximum value and begins to decrease.

(8) If the decrease below the maximum introduced by final cut is not more than a few milliamps, the set can now be connected permanently to the feeder at this point. If a large decrease in feeder current was made by the final cut, replace the last few inches of feeder, tape the joins and connect in the set.

NOTES

3, 4, 5 and 6 of previous method apply.

It will, of course, be realized that the aerial system will work at maximum efficiency only on the one channel for which the system has been tuned. On a normal installation, however, with a total length of about 60 feet of feeder, the system should remain quite efficient over about 10 W.S. 31 channels, five on either side of the channel to which the system is tuned. The rate of efficiency decrease on either side of the selected channel is greater the longer the feeder, and for this reason and also because of losses in the feeder itself, the set should be kept as close as possible to the aerial installation.

10. **The Vehicle Aerial.**—The vehicle aerial for use on the move is merely a whip aerial of about 11 feet in length. The method of end-feeding to whips is, however, slightly different from the usual Army practice; this difference is introduced so that the whip section can be employed also as part of the better aerial used when the vehicle is stationary.

The aerial for use when the vehicle is stationary and better signals than those available from the usual whip aerial are desired, consists of a driven element and a parasitic reflector. When properly working it should give a gain of 4-5 dbs over the whip aerial. Since it has a directional pattern of radiation it must be mounted in such a way that it can be rotated through 360 degrees so that it can be directed on to the station being worked.

The aerial consists essentially of a half-wave end-fed rod with a reflector cut to such a length that the phase of the current induced in it effectively increases the strength of the radiation in one direction while decreasing it in others. The formulae for the length of the two elements are:—

$$\text{Length of driven element} = \frac{475 \text{ ft.}}{\text{Frequency in megacycles}}$$

$$\text{Length of reflector} = \frac{500 \text{ ft.}}{\text{Frequency in megacycles}}$$

The two whips are mounted in aerial bases No. 10 or No. 11 at a distance apart equal to one-tenth of a wavelength.

$$\text{Separation} = \frac{\text{Wavelength}}{10} = \frac{98.5 \text{ ft.}}{\text{Frequency in megacycles}}$$

The two whips are mounted on a cross-arm which should be non-metallic. Ideally, a good insulating material should be used, but seasoned timber is satisfactory. Through the centre of the cross-arm, and at right angles to it is fixed a rod (which may be of metal) which forms the axle on which the array rotates.

An aerial mounting bracket No. 5 forms a convenient means of attaching the aerial to the vehicle. It is only a small engineering job to modify this to take the aerial. The mounting can be designed so that the aerial lifts out when not required, leaving the No. 11 base free for the whip aerial to be used on the move. Alternatively, the mounting can be fixed in position, and a clamp can be designed, so that for working on the move the reflector can be taken out, and the driven element remains to act as the normal whip.

Figure 5 gives the general appearance of the aerial. Figure 5 (A) shows the removable version, while 5 (B) shows the version in which the reflector only is removed for mobile working. A suitable clamp to prevent movement of the cross-arm will have to be designed.

11. **Driving the Aerial.**—The driven element is fed through twin transmission line. At the set end, the wires are connected to aerial and earth on the set. At the top end of the feeder, the lead going to the set aerial is connected to the driven element, while that going to earth on the set is left free. For tuning, the aerial side of the transmission line is cut for the radio frequency meter and tuning is carried out exactly as described for the static elevated aerial. With K24 feeder, the feeder length will be of the order of 6-8 feet. The tuning may also, of course, be carried out using a modified W.S. 31 as a field strength meter. Maximum field strength should be found to occur along the line of the cross-arm in the direction reflector-driven element.

The same piece of feeder may be used to feed the single whip aerial. The matching will not be perfect, but the loss of signal strength should be small. If the utmost is required from the whip aerial, a separate twin wire feeder can be cut for it.

Note.—This method of feeding the aerial will be recognized by many as the well-known "Zepp" feed.

The directional qualities and the gain of this aerial will not be obvious when working on strong signals, when the limiting action of the F.M. sets will hide the effects. The characteristics should clearly be seen, however, when working on signals which are of about strength 1 on the normal whip aerial. When working a net of stations the aerial must, of course, be pointed at the station working at the moment.

ANNEXURE I
MODIFICATION TO PERMIT USE OF W.S. 31 AS FIELD-STRENGTH METER

Summary

1. The modification to enable the W.S. 31 to be used as a field-strength meter is very simple and does not in any way affect the set performance. The grid current in the first limiter valve (V12) is used as an indication of received signal strength.

Details of Modification

2. Remove resister R42 (1 M) which is connected between the grid (pin 6) of V12, and a tag strip connected to socket 2 on the octal test socket at the side of the set chassis.

3. Replace the resister by a 100 K component of similar rating.

4. Connect leads to sockets 2 and 8 (earth) on the left socket, and bring these out of the set case for connexion to a suitable meter.

5. The meter should read 0–100 milliamp for preference, but anything up to 0–500 milliamp f.s.d. could be used.

Operation of the Field-strength Meter

6. Connect a short length of wire (2–3 inches) to the aerial of the 31 set.

CAUTION.—*Do Not Operate the "SEND" Pressel Switch with the Meter Connected.*

7. Set up the "field-strength meter" about 100 yards from the set and the aerial system under investigation. Switch on the "field-strength meter" and with the set under test switched to "send", observe the reading on the meter.

8. Adjust your distance from the transmitting aerial system until the meter reads some convenient figure, say 30–50 milliamps.

9. The system is now ready to be used for comparative tests on the set and aerial system; adjustments to which should be made until the meter reading shows a maximum.

NOTES

It will be observed that any movement in the vicinity of the "field-strength meter" will cause fluctuations in the readings. Operators should assume the same positions in relation to the short test aerial when making each reading.

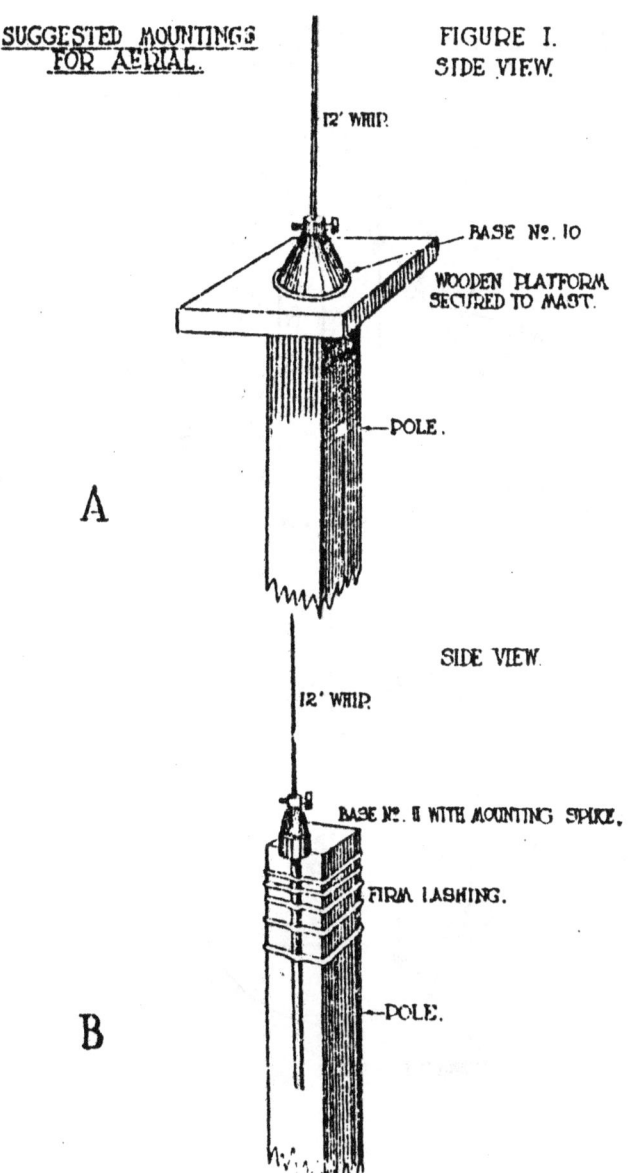

SUGGESTED MOUNTINGS FOR AERIAL.

FIGURE I.
SIDE VIEW.

12' WHIP.

BASE No. 10

WOODEN PLATFORM SECURED TO MAST.

POLE.

A

SIDE VIEW.

12' WHIP.

BASE No. 11 WITH MOUNTING SPIKE.

FIRM LASHING.

POLE.

B

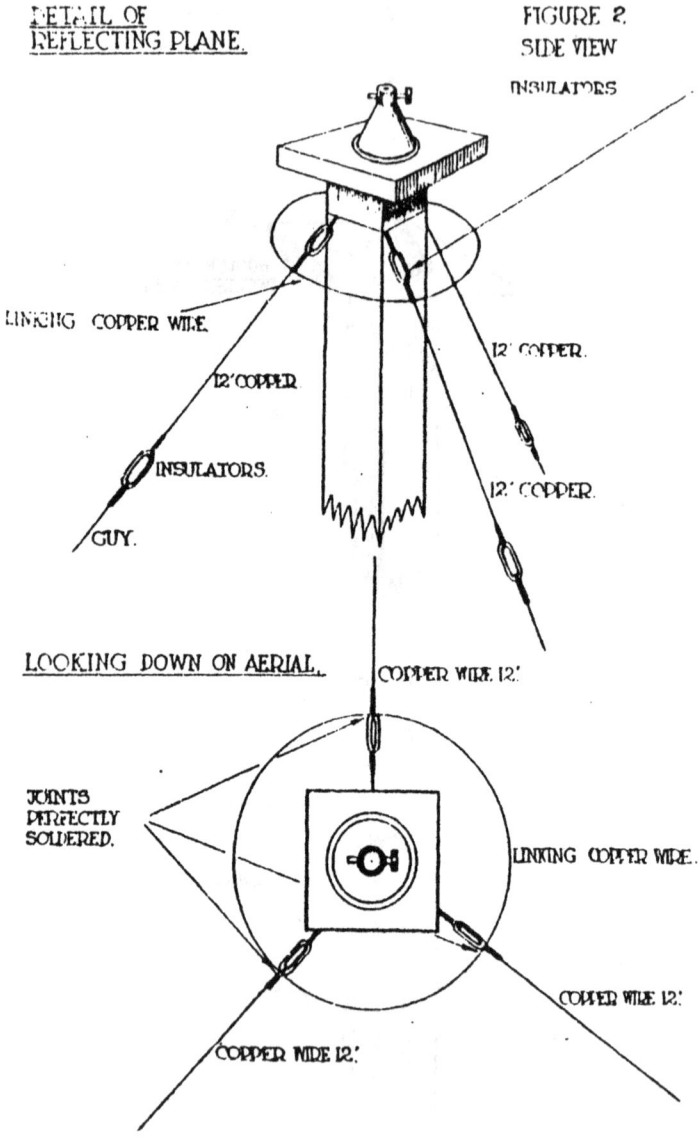

FEEDER CONNECTIONS. FIGURE 5.

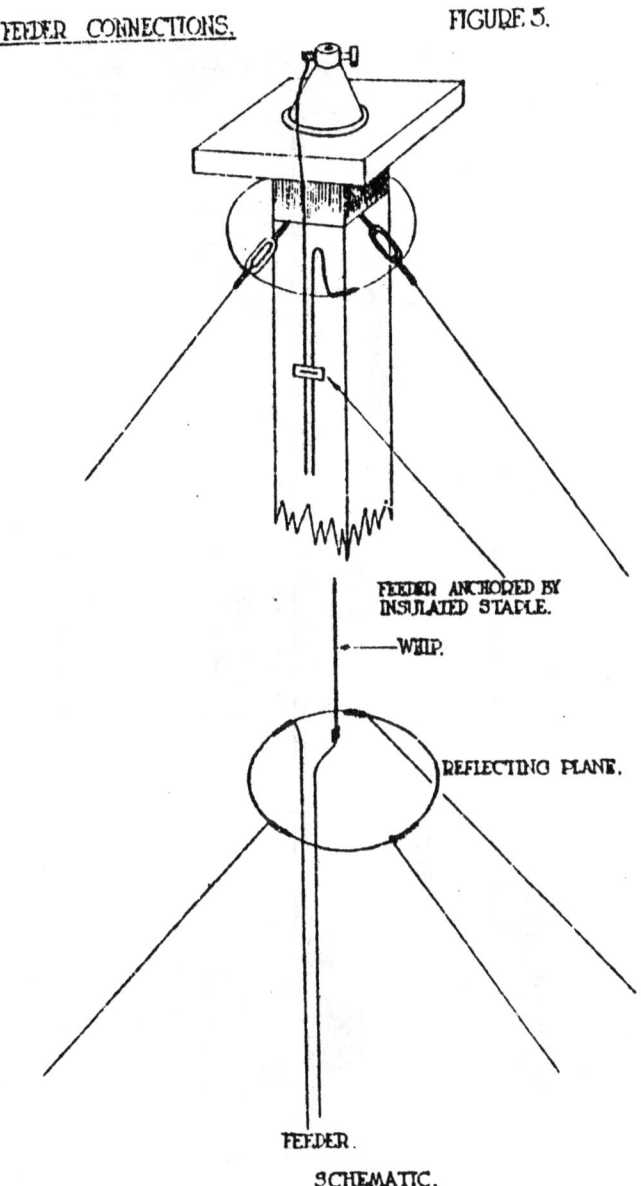

FEEDER ANCHORED BY INSULATED STAPLE.
— WHIP.
REFLECTING PLANE.
FEEDER.
SCHEMATIC.

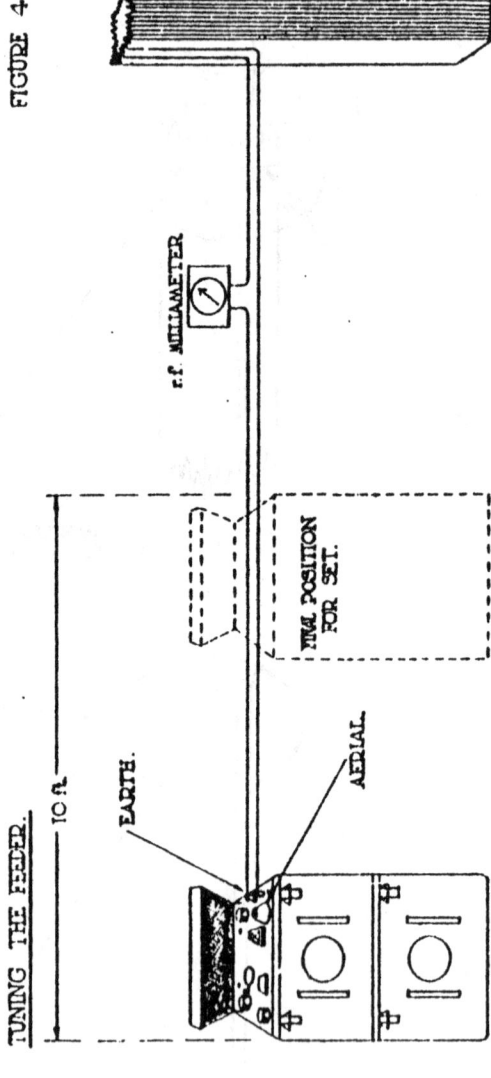

FIGURE 4

TUNING THE FEEDER.

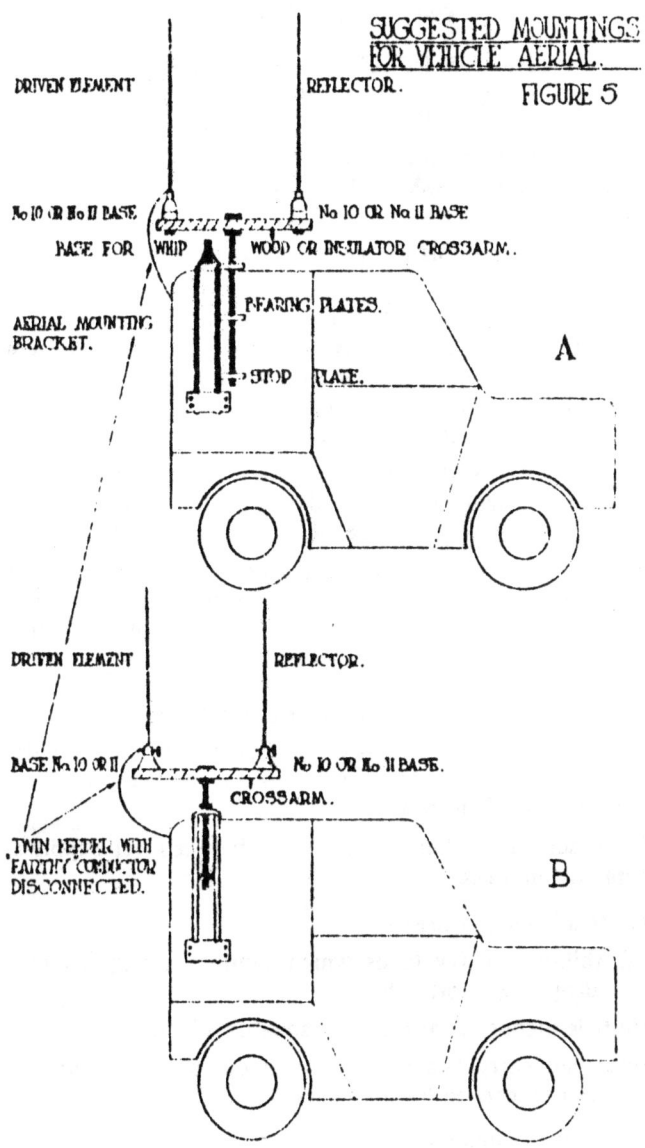

CHAPTER XVIII

THE USE OF ANIMAL TRANSPORT

Section 1—General

1. There is at present in Kenya, one animal transport company (67 A.T. Coy. E.A.A.S.C.), with a total of 144 load-carrying animals. This company fulfils the pack transport requirements of the three brigades.

2. When it is realized that the normal allocation of Animal Transport for front line duties is 72 animals per battalion it will at once be obvious that there is the greatest need for economy in demanding pack transport, and that at all times it must be operated with the greatest efficiency.

3. The shortage of British manpower in the Animal Transport company usually results in detachments of animals being sent out to battalions in charge of an African N.C.O.

4. This means that the onus for supervising all aspects of the work of the detachment devolves on the battalion officers and men and they must, therefore, acquire a much wider experience of pack transport than is usually necessary.

Section 2—Uses and Limitations

5. The sole function of pack transport is to carry loads in country which is unsuitable for wheeled transport, e.g. the forests and high moorland of Kenya.

In the scheme of things it thus fits in between jeep supply and air supply or man pack.

6. Its advantages are:—

(*a*) Ability to carry loads which cannot be supplied by air drop, e.g. mortar bombs.

(*b*) It is inconspicuous and reasonably silent.

(*c*) It can carry heavier and more cumbersome loads than can be carried by man pack.

7. Its disadvantages are:—

(*a*) It is slow.

(b) It is limited by the fatigue of animals and drivers.

(c) It is dependent on water supplies.

(d) The load capacity may be reduced by the necessity of carrying forage.

(e) It is uneconomical—one 3-tonner will carry as much as 40 mules.

Section 3—Responsibilities

8. Battalions which have a detachment of pack animals attached to them have certain very definite responsibilities. These are:—

(a) The provision of water and forage for the animals, the selection of a suitable site for their accommodation and the provision of a breast line. (*See* Section 9.)

(b) The provision of accommodation and food for the drivers.

(c) The provision of trained loading and unloading parties. (*See* Section 6.)

(d) The provision of guides and escorts.

(e) The clearance of paths for the animals where big game tracks do not exist. (*Note*: a loaded horse or mule requires a clearance of 6 ft. wide and 6 ft. high.)

(f) The supervision of the care and general management of the animals.

Section 4—Employment

9. Battalions must give as much warning as possible to the N.C.O. i/c animals before they are required to move in order that he can arrange watering and feeding prior to saddling up.

10. Animals should not be loaded in rear of the most forward point which can reached by mechanical transport.

11. Loads should be worked out, prepared ready for loading, and set out in loading lanes. Account must be taken of any forage it may be necessary to take.

12. Watering points must be thought out.

13. Loading parties, guides, escorts, etc., must be provided.

Section 5—The Fitting of Pack Saddles

14. Men must understand how to fit pack saddles so that they can do a quick check before loading.

Badly fitting saddles and incorrect loading result in injuries to the animals backs—the greatest cause of wastage in Animal Transport companies.

15. The principles of saddle fitting are very simple:—

   (a) The saddle must be wide enough to avoid pinching the top of the shoulder.

   (b) No weight must press on the spine.

   (c) The shoulder blades must not have their free movement restricted by the front of the saddle.

   (d) Weight must not rest on the loins.

   (e) The weight must rest on top of the ribs and must be evenly distributed over the surface which extends from behind the play of the shoulder blade to the last rib.

16. It is particularly important to check the folding of the saddle blanket, which should be done in such a way as to avoid weight being transmitted to the withers and spine through the tightness of the blanket. Pulling up the blanket where it rests on the spine in such a way as to form a "channel" will obviate this.

Section 6—Roping and Loading

17. The technique of roping and loading can only be acquired by practice. Battalions should arrange for representatives from the Animal Transport Company to give instruction in this subject, and follow up the instruction with adequate practice periods.

18. The principles of loading are:—

   (a) The load should be carried as far as possible over the tops of the ribs and as little as possible over the sides of them. Every endeavour should be made to avoid compressing the sides, for not only is the load carried at a disadvantage if placed low down, but it interferes with the animal's breathing—an important factor at high altitudes.

(b) A very high load on the other hand is bad as it tends to sway.

(c) Loads cannot be too flat; the flatter they are the closer they lie to the saddle. This means that the animal requires less room to move in forest paths, and is less liable to fatigue or injury to the back.

(d) The load must not touch the animal. If it extends in front or behind the saddle it must still be kept clear of the shoulders or hips.

(e) Girths and surcingle must be tight.

(f) The load must be balanced. Therefore the hanging of rifles, haversacks, etc., on the saddle must be strictly forbidden. Even a difference of 5 lb. in the weight of each side will increase the risk of injury. So important is load equilibrium that it may be necessary to add a small bag of sand to the light side to ensure balance.

(g) The load must not be kept on the animals back longer than necessary. If the distance to be covered is a long one there must be halts from time to time when the animals can be off-saddled. This will avoid injuries due to constant pressure. As a general rule loaded saddles should not be on the animal for longer than four hours at a stretch.

19. The pack animals will carry a load of approximately 160 lb., which must be divided into two halves of equal size and weight. Loads should, where possible, be roped on the ground, and then hung on the saddle loading hooks and secured by a surcingle. This is preferable to lashing the load to the saddle.

20. Loads should always be capable of rapid and simple adjustment and, as far as possible, only knots which can be undone with one pull of the rope should be used.

21. The use of Universal Carriers (slatted wooden carriers on the Venetian blind principle) will be of assistance for awkward loads, or when men are inadequately trained. Panniers of leather, canvas, or basket work are also of assistance.

22. The loads, when prepared, should be laid on the ground in lanes. Lanes should be 6 ft. wide, with an interval of 5 ft. between each pair of loads.

23. The animals are led into the lane, each stopping opposite its allotted load. The loading party then simultaneously hang each half load on to the loading hooks of the saddles and secure them. It is important that this be done simultaneously to avoid the saddle being pulled over to one side.

Section 7—Loads

24. The more common loads which Battalions will require the animals to carry are dealt with as follows:—

(a) Compo.

Each box weighs 40 lb. Load therefore is two boxes per side in universal carriers.

(b) 3 in. Mortar

The barrel and spare parts are carried in a universal carrier and is one side load (weight 45 lb.).

The bipod (weight 44½ lb.) form the other side load and is roped to the saddle. (A pad needs to be placed between the bipod and the saddle to prevent injury to the animal from the spikes on the bipod.)

The base plate (weight 37 lb.) is loaded last and forms the top load. It is secured by a strap or surcingle.

(c) Mortar Bombs

Twelve bombs in their boxes can be carried, six each side. The boxes may either be lashed to the saddle or they can be put into Bags, entrenching tool, which are used as panniers and will be supplied by the Animal Transport Company on demand.

(d) M.M.G.

Gun and water should be loaded as follows:—
Near Side.—Tripod (50 lb.).
Offside.—Two gallons of water in tins (25 lb.) and makeweight, e.g. Sand.
Topside.—Gun (32 lb.).
Place baggage ropes on the saddle hooks.

Place two pick helves or similar pieces of wood across the baggage ropes and secure by double half hitches. The helves should be about two inches apart. Tie the side loads on to pick helves. Crosshead of tripod should be upwards and legs to rear.

(e) Wireless Sets

All wireless sets can be carried, the set itself being one side-load, the batteries the other, and head pieces, spare parts, etc., being carried as a top load.

Sets and batteries can be carried in bags, entrenching tool or universal carriers.

Care must be taken to ensure that the set is not damaged in narrow paths.

With only minor modifications the set can be operated whilst on the animal.

Battalions intending to use animals to carry wireless sets should tell the Animal Transport Company in order that they can provide a big, quiet animal.

Weights of sets are as follows.

W.S. 22	38 lb.
Power Supply Unit	21 lb.
W.S 62	29 lb.
W.S. 19 (with P.S.U.)	88 lb.
Battery secondary portable 12v.–22A.H.	35 lb.
Charging set 80 watt	53 lb.
Charging set 300 watt	80 lb.

Full loading details for W.S. 22 and 62, Animal Pack, are contained in the following pamphlets:—

Wireless Sets No. 22—Animal Pack—Loading and Fitting.
W.O. Code 1060.

Wireless Stations No. 62—Animal Park from Pack Fitting and Loading Instructions.
Z.A. 27865.

Section 8—March Discipline

25. The driver leads two animals, the second being fastened by a rope from its head-collar to the back of the saddle of the leader.

In difficult going it may be necessary to uncouple the animals, in which case the employing unit will have to provide the additional men required to lead the animals.

26. The animal's pace is a walk. Only in emergency should he be made to trot when carrying a saddle.

At the walk he will, in open country, cover $2\frac{1}{2}$-$3\frac{1}{2}$ miles per hour, with a daily total mileage of about 20.

In the forest progress will, of course, be much slower.

27. The secret of leading animals is to allow them as much freedom as possible. The animal must be allowed to pick his own path and his head must be free so that he can balance himself.

Men must not fall into the common trap of trying to tow the animal along. If he is reluctant to move forward, or does so too slowly, persuasion should be applied from the rear. If an animal, who is normally willing, is reluctant to move forward do not urge it before making a proper investigation. There may be something wrong with its load or it may have gone lame.

28. Whilst on the march a close watch must be kept on the loads. Escorting infantry must be prepared to go at once to the assistance of an animal whose load shows signs of slipping.

29. The hanging of rifles or other equipment on the animals must be forbidden, and on no account whatsoever should men be allowed to ride.

30. During the march, there should be a short halt soon after starting in order to check and adjust loads. Thereafter there should be a halt for about 10 minutes every hour, or more frequently if the going is very difficult. Every four hours there should be a long halt when the animals are off-loaded and unsaddled. When this is done all animals should be carefully examined for sign of injury.

31. Watering should take place wherever the opportunity offers. Animals will not suffer from being allowed to drink whilst on the march.

32. Should an animal slip and fall whilst on the march, the load and saddle must be removed before attempting to get it up.

Section 9—Care of Animals

33. The management of horses and mules is not difficult, being very largely a matter of common sense, keen observation, and a capacity for taking pains.

34. In each battalion there will be men who have the necessary experience and keenness. A short attachment to the Animal Transport Company will ensure the training of others.

General Management

35. Camp Sites for the animals should be selected with the following points in mind:—

(a) Proximity to water.

(b) Avoidance of stony, uneven ground: a horse, like a man, wants to lie down after a hard day.

(c) Protection from the weather. A horse or mule will not do well if he spends his days being pestered by flies under a blazing sun—shade and breeze are desirable. Similarly, during the rainy season, the lines should be sited to give the animal what shelter is possible from driving rain.

36. Animals in camp are best secured by their headropes to a taut strong rope fastened breast high between trees or posts. Animals should be fastened on alternate sides of the rope with 6 ft. between each animal. They should not be fastened to such things as barbed wire fences, 3-tonners, etc.

37. Lines should be kept as clean as possible and all manure removed or buried: failure to do so will attract flies.

38. Grooming is unnecessary. Only mud, dirt, and sweat marks need be removed with a dandy brush.

39. Feet should be examined regularly for loose shoes, stones, etc., and arrangements should be made for the Animal Transport Company to send farriers, once per month, to shoe all animals.

Watering

40. A horse or mule requires from 8–12 gallons per day, and when not on the march should be watered at least three times per day.

41. Plenty of time must be allowed for the animal to drink. At all times the bit must be removed before drinking and, if on the march, loads should be removed and girths slackened.

42. Both horses and mules are creatures of habit, particularly where drinking is concerned. Thus a mule accustomed to drink from running water may be reluctant to drink from a bucket—patience is required to induce him to do so.

43. An adequate supply of clean, fresh water at all times is essential to the health and condition of the animal.

Feeding

44. It is the responsibility of the user unit, not the Animal Transport Company, to feed animals which are attached to the battalion.

45. The ration in Kenya is:—

	Horses and Mules over 13.2	Horses and Mules under 13.2
Hay	14 lb.	10 lb.
Grain	8 lb.	5 lb.
Salt	1 oz.	1 oz.

Full details can be obtained in the pamphlet "Ration Scales East Africa".

46. The ration of grain should always be drawn. Hay need only be drawn at certain times of the year when no grass or hay is growing locally.

47. The animals will be sent out by the Animal Transport Company with a nosebag and a haynet. Nosebags are used for the grain feed and need to be kept clean. After each feed they should be turned inside out and allowed to dry. Haynets should always be used. The haynet should be packed as tightly as possible with hay. Each animal will need two filled nets per day.

48. The principle of feeding horses and mules is to:—

(a) Water before feed.

(b) Feed little and often.

49. Every effort should be made to get animals out to graze.

Exercise

50. Regular daily exercise is most important. When not being used animals should do a regular two hours each day, carrying pack saddles and loads. Only after a particularly arduous march should they be allowed to stand in.

51. No pack animal must be exercised by being ridden.

Section 10—Carriage of Animals by Road

52. Animals will normally be collected from the Animal Transport Company in unit 3-tonners.

53. As a guide it may be taken that a 3-tonner will carry four pack animals loaded head to tail across the truck, together with their saddlery, drivers and kit.

54. The carriage of animals in mechanical transport calls for great care on the part of the driver:—

(a) Only skilled drivers should be used and they should be ordered to drive slowly particularly round corners and on rough roads.

(b) Canopies are essential.

(c) Where possible, vehicles with wheel boxes or projecting fittings should not be used.

(d) Spare wheels, petrol, oil, etc., must not be carried in the body of the vehicle.

(e) If the floor is of metal, it should be covered with earth or litter.

(f) Animals are loaded by backing the vehicle against a convenient bank and off-loaded in the same way.

(g) When loading and unloading, care is necessary to ensure that any gaps, holes, etc., in the tailboard are filled with straw, earth, litter or wood.

(h) Drivers accompanying the animals should always travel in the back of the truck to look after them. The driver or co-driver should keep his eye on what is happening in the back and should at once stop if anything shows signs of going wrong.

Section 11—Care of Sick and Injured

55. All injuries due to saddles, loads, etc., are preventable and should not happen.

56. Should, however, the services of a veterinary officer be required, the drill is:—

   (a) If near NANYUKI, ring up the Animal Transport Company, state what is wrong, and ask for assistance.

   (b) If away from NANYUKI, contact the nearest civilian veterinary surgeon.

   In addition, there are Government Veterinary surgeons or livestock officers at the following places:—

Veterinary Officers	Livestock Officers
MACHAKOS	MOLO
NYERI	EMBU
NANYUKI	ISIOLO
NARO MORU	MERU
THOMSON'S FALLS	FORT HALL
LIMURU	THIKA
GILGIL	KIRUI
NAKURU	NAIVASHA

   (c) Bills from Civilian Veterinary Surgeons, together with a signed A.F.P. 1922, should be forwarded to D.A.D.V. and R.S. General Headquarters, P.O. Box 4000, Nairobi, when payment will be arranged.

57. In simple cases of injury, etc., obtain the advice of your unit Medical Officer pending the arrival of a veterinary surgeon.

58. Should it be necessary to destroy an animal as a result of incurable injury, e.g. broken leg, this should be done with a pistol. The point at which to aim is where two imaginary lines, each from the base of one ear to the inner corner of the opposite eye, intersect.

59. The death or destruction of any animals should be reported to Officer Commanding, Animal Transport Company, who will advise units on the necessary write-off procedure.

Section 12—Conclusion

60. Battalions will find animal transport invaluable in supplying isolated detachments or for accompanying long range forest patrols.

61. All companies should aim at having at least one officer or N.C.O. who has sufficient experience of animal transport to be able to supervise its use, and all should have a sufficient number of men trained in tying and loading.

Short courses can be arranged at the Animal Transport Company, and occasionally instructors can be attached from the Animal Transport Company to teach on the spot.

62. Failures with animal transport are invariably due to ignorance which can be avoided by proper instruction and a clear understanding by all of the uses and limitations.

CHAPTER XIX

OPERATIONAL SUPPLY

Section 1—Operational Rations

Introduction

1. It must always be the aim to feed the man with fresh food, but if, for operational reasons, this is not possible, tinned rations must be used instead.

2. The Messing Officer or Quartermaster in charge of rations must bear in mind that patrols may well be called out at very short notice and, in order to avoid wastage of fresh rations drawn but unsuitable for the patrol, a proportion of compo rations should be to hand.

3. Rations for patrols should be of the minimum weight and those which require little or no preparation before consumption. The compo pack, as it stands, is bulky and experience has found that the individual on patrol does not have the same inclination for food at heights of 10,000 feet, especially if he has to carry it. Invariably men will carry as little food as possible, leaving the balance to be eaten on their return. They like biscuits, corned beef, cheese, raisins, chocolate, tea, sugar and milk, which works out at 3 lb. per man per day or 12 lb. per man for a 4-day patrol.

4. **Preparation of Patrol Meals.**—Cooking can either be by individual mess tin cooking or by messing centrally. Before resorting to individual mess tin cooking it is well to remember the following points:—

Individual mess tin cooking: —

(a) Takes longer than central cooking.

(b) Requires most of your patrol to be engaged in cooking when they might be resting or on guard.

(c) Involves a number of small fires.

5. **Types of Rations.**—The following types of rations and packs are available in East Africa. (*See* Appendix "A" for general data.)

TYPE OF RATION:—

British	Compo	*See* Appendix "B"
	24-hour	*See* Appendix "C"
African	Scale 9	*See* Appendix "D"
Ancillaries	Self-heating beverages	
	Hexamine cookers	*See* Appendix "E"
	Rum/tea	

6. **Compo. Pack.**—The 10-men composite pack normally referred to as "Compo" is designed for party or bulk feeding where it is not possible to issue normal fresh rations or tinned rations. This pack is available in seven types marked "A", "B", "C", "D", "E", "F" or "G".

7. **24-hour Pack.**—Europeans serving with African troops can draw the 24-hour pack which is designed for individual feeding where bulk or party feeding is impossible. This pack is not designed for prolonged use. There are three types, namely "A", "B" and "C".

8. **Issues of Compo. Packs.**—Issues of packs shown in paragraphs 6 and 7 above, will be varied by the Supply Depot/Composite Platoon.

9. **Method of Distribution.**—Supplies may be drawn from 70 Supply Depot, Nanyuki, 111 Composite Platoon, Nyeri, or 37 Supply Depot, Kahawa near Nairobi. Should the trend of operations require it, a supply point will be opened at set times near the forward troops.

10. **Accounting.**—Detailed instructions on accounting are contained in "R.A.S.C. STANDING ORDERS IN EAST AFRICA".

Section 2—P.O.L.

11. Vehicle petrol may be obtained from any of the several Petrol Points established within the theatre. All larger units in addition, are required to establish a domestic petrol point operating with 44 gallon drums with a Malco pump or by jerrican.

12. Lubricants will be obtained from a Supply Depot, normally on a monthly basis.

13. Detailed instructions are contained in General Headquarters East Africa Administrative Instruction No. 20 "Administration in Operational Areas".

Section 3—Means of Delivery

14. **Methods.**—Delivery of supplies is effected by one of the following means:—

(a) 3-ton vehicle.

(b) Jeeps/Land Rovers.

(c) Animal Transport.

(d) Porters.

(e) Air supply.

15. Normally supplies and P.O.L. are collected from supply depots or supply points by unit 3-ton vehicles. During the long and short rains in Kenya, minor roads or tracks quickly become impassable to anything but light 4 x 4 vehicles, and Jeeps and Land Rovers have to be used up to roadheads. Any maintenance forward of roadhead must be carried out by some other means such as animal transport, porterage or air supply.

16. **Animal Transport.**—An Animal Transport Company exists, with its base at Nanyuki. It is made up of Company Headquarters and three modified troops, a total of 144 animals. The carrying capacity of each animal (mule and pack pony) is 160 lb. (4 x 10 men compo packs).

17. **Porterage.**—Porters are used for the carriage of supplies where it is impossible for animal transport to penetrate the jungle. Again these porters have their obvious limitations as load carriers.

Section 4—Air Supply

18. **Introduction.**—Supply by air is normally carried out by light aircraft by "free" drop. This may be supplemented by parachute drop.

19. **Free Drop by Light Aircraft.**—Demands for drops by light aircraft for small patrols will be made through Brigade Headquarters to Ground Liaison Officer, Nyeri. These demands must be made 24 hours in advance.

20. **Parachute Drop by R.A.F.**—The only occasions when parachute drops are made are in pre-planned operations. The necessary plans are made by the brigades concerned in conjunction with the Joint Operations Centre.

21. Demands for rations will automatically be met by compo packs for British and Scale 9 (with rice) for Africans. The packs include 20 per cent extra for small party feeding. Special requirements must be clearly stated.

22. Daily U.K. and local papers will be dropped as available.

23. Det. 73 Coy. R.A.S.C. (Air Despatch) is prepared to drop any supplies or amenities which the unit can arrange.

24. **Ammunition will NOT be dropped by any means.**

APPENDIX "A" TO CHAPTER XIX
RATIONS—GENERAL DATA—OPERATIONAL

Type of Ration	Details of Packing	Gross Weight One Pack	Gross Weight One Ration	Food Value (Calories)
British Compo.	10 rations (without biscuit) in wood or fibre box 16½" x 10¾" x 10"	42 lb.	3 lb. 2 oz.	4,200 with biscuit
Biscuits Service	3 tins x 11 lb. per box 31" x 11¾" x 10¼"	51 lb.	9 oz. Total weight of ration 3 lb. 11 oz.	
British 24 hour pack ..	10 rations in sealed tin carton inside fibre box	50 lb.	3¾ lb.	3,900
A.O.R. Scale 9. 5-man pack for		—	4 lb.	4,366
free drop Scale 9		26 lb.	4 lb.	4,366

APPENDIX "B" TO CHAPTER XIX
Composition of the British Composite Ration Pack
(10 Men)

Notes

(1) For variety, these packs are produced in seven types (A, B, C, D, E, F and G).

(2) Bread should be consumed where possible (scale 12 oz.) or biscuits may be drawn (scale 9 oz.).

(3) Packs E, F and G are now in production but are not yet in use in this theatre.

Commodity and Type of Container	Net Contents Per Can	A	B	C	D	E	F	G
No. 1 TALL CANS:								
Oatmeal Blocks	10 × 1 oz.	1	1	1	—	—	1	—
Bacon	15 oz.	3	—	—	—	—	1	—
Sausage	15 oz.	—	3	—	—	—	2	—
Ham and Eggs	15 oz.	—	—	3	—	—	—	3
Bacon and Beans	16 oz.	—	—	—	3	—	—	—
Sausage and Beans	16 oz.	—	—	—	—	3	—	—
Tea	6 oz.	1	1	1	1	1	1	1
Sugar	14½ oz.	1	1	1	1	1	1	1
Stewed Steak	16 oz.	—	6	—	—	—	—	—
Steak and Kidney Pudding	16 oz.	—	—	6	—	—	—	—
Meat and Vegetables	16 oz.	—	—	—	10	—	—	—
Irish Stew	16 oz.	—	—	—	—	10	—	—
Casserole Steak and Onions	16 oz.	—	—	—	—	—	6	—
Mutton, Scotch Style	16 oz.	—	—	—	—	—	—	10
Peas	10 oz.	—	1	1	—	—	—	—
Beans	16 oz.	—	—	—	—	—	1	—
Diced Mixed Vegetables	10 oz.	—	—	1	—	—	—	—
Carrots	10 oz.	—	1	—	—	—	1	—
Vegetable Salad in Mayonnaise	15 oz.	2	—	—	—	—	—	—
Potato Mash Powder	11 oz.	1	1	1	—	—	1	—
Treacle Pudding	14 oz.	—	3	—	—	—	—	—
Rice Pudding	16 oz.	—	—	3	—	—	—	—
Jam Roll Pudding	15 oz.	—	—	—	3	—	—	—
Ginger Pudding	14 oz.	—	—	—	—	3	—	—
Apple Pudding	15 oz.	—	—	—	—	—	—	3
Luncheon Meat	16 oz.	—	2	—	—	—	2	—
Hamburgers	16 oz.	—	—	2	—	—	—	—
Rich Cake	10 oz.	—	—	—	2	—	—	—
Ham and Beef	16 oz.	—	—	—	—	2	—	2
Chocolate and Sweets:								
Chocolate	5 × 2 oz.	2	2	2	2	—	2	—
Sweets	2½ oz.							
Raisin Chocolate	5 × 2 oz.	—	—	—	—	2	—	2
Clear Gums	2½ oz.							

Commodity and Type of Container	Net Contents per Can	Type and Number of Cans						
		A	B	C	D	E	F	G
Matches	1 Box (47)							
Water Sterilising Outfit	1 Tin							
Salt Dispenser	1 × 2 oz.	1	1	1	1	1	1	1
Paludrine	19 Tablets							
A. 1 TALL CANS:								
Fruit Canned	16 oz.	3	—	—	—	—	3	—
Salmon	16 oz.	2	—	—	—	—	—	—
½—A.1 TALL CANS:								
Sugar	7 oz.	1	1	1	1	1	1	1
Sweets	5 oz.	1	1	1	1	—	1	—
Clear Gums	5 oz.	—	—	—	—	1	—	1
Cheese, Processed	8 oz.	2	2	2	2	2	2	2
Margarine	7¼ oz.	2	2	2	2	2	2	2
Jam	9 oz.	2	1	2	1	2	1	2
Marmalade	9 oz.	—	1	—	1	—	1	—
300 × 111 CANS:								
Tea	1½ oz.	1	1	1	1	1	1	1
Sugar	4 oz.	1	1	1	1	1	1	1
VARIOUS:								
Preserved Meat	12 oz.	6	—	—	—	—	—	—
Milk Condensed, Unsweetened	8 oz.	4	4	4	4	4	4	4
Latrine Paper — In	100 pieces							
Can Opener — Waxed	1 No.	1	1	1	1	1	1	1
Contents List — Bag	1 No.							
Soap G.P.	1 Tablet	1	1	1	1	1	1	1
Reclosure Lids	—	2	2	2	2	2	2	2

APPENDIX "C" TO CHAPTER XIX

Composition of the British One-man 24-hour Ration, for Europeans with African Troops

(Pack Made in Three Types— A, B and C)

This ration is packed into three separate meals, plus a Sundries Packet as under.

Commodity	Quantity ozs.	Type of Pack		
		A	B	C
Breakfast Meal:				
Oatmeal Block	1 oz	1	1	1
Chopped Bacon	5 oz.	1	—	—
Bacon and Beans	5¼ oz.	—	1	—
Sausage and Beans	5¼ oz.	—	—	1
Jam	2 oz.	1	—	1
Marmalade	2 oz.	—	1	—
Tea	¼ oz.	1	1	1
Sugar..	1 oz.	1	1	1
Biscuits, Service	3 oz.	1	1	1
Snack Meal:				
Milk Choclate	2 oz.	1	1	1
Clear Gums	1⅛ oz.	1	1	1
Spangees	1½ oz.	1	—	—
Butt-o-Scotch	1¾ oz.	—	1	—
Boiled Sweets	2 oz.	—	—	1
Mars Bar	1⅛ oz.	1	—	—
Boiled Sweets	2 oz.	—	1	—
Nuts and Raisins	1½ oz.	—	—	1
Biscuits, Sweet	3 oz.	1	1	1
Tea	¼ oz.	1	1	1
Sugar	1 oz.	1	1	1
Main Meal:				
Corned Beef	5 oz.	1	—	—
Ham and Beef	5 oz.	—	1	—
Liver and Bacon	5¼ oz.	—	—	1
Vegetable Salad in Mayonnaise ..	4 oz.	1	—	—
Spaghetti	5¼ oz.	—	1	—
Beans in Tomato	5 oz.	—	—	1
Mixed Fruit Pudding	4 oz.	1	—	—
Treacle Pudding	3½ oz.	—	1	—
Rice Pudding	5 oz.	—	—	1
Cheese	1½ oz.	1	1	1
Biscuits, Service	3 oz.	1	1	1
Tea	¼ oz.	1	1	1
Sugar..	1 oz.	1	1	1
Sundries:				
Condensed Milk (Tube)	2 oz.	1	1	1
Salt in Dispenser	5½ gms.	1	1	1
Chewing Gum	4 Tablets	1	1	1
Matches (Book)	1 No.	1	1	1
Paludrine Tablet	1 No.	1	1	1
Toilet Paper	10 Sheets	1	1	1
Can Opener	1 No.	1	1	1
Contents List				

APPENDIX "D" TO CHAPTER XIX

Composition of the African Operational Scale No. 9

This is not a special pack but is designed to meet the need of the Askari with the minimum of preparation.

This scale is produced as a five-man pack for free drop by air, in which case items are contained in grease-proof paper bags within cotton bags.

The five-man pack contains five rations made up to the nearest tin and does NOT include any authorized percentage for small numbers.

Item	Scale for 1 Ration	Scale for 5 men air pack	Remarks
Rice (Unpolished)	12 oz.	60 oz.	
Meat Preserved MK	6 oz.	30 oz.	3x 12 oz. cans
Vit Ghee Sub	1¼ oz.	6¼ oz.	1x6¼ oz. cans
Vegetables, Tinned	4 oz.	Nil	
Beans, canned	4 oz.	40 oz.	3x16 oz. cans
Dates, Pitted	6 oz.	30 oz.	4x½ lb pkts. or 2x1 lb. packets
Groundnuts, without Shell ..	4½ oz.	22½ oz.	
Fruit, Dried	1 oz.	5 oz.	
Sugar	2½ oz.	12½ oz.	
Salt Coarse	¾ oz.	3¾ oz.	
Tea	½ oz.	2½ oz.	
Curry Powder	1/16 oz.	5/16 oz.	
Biscuits	4½ oz.	22½ oz.	
Milk Tinned	2 oz.	10 oz.	1x16 oz. cans

APPENDIX "E" TO CHAPTER XIX
Ancillaries for Use by Operational Troops

Self-heating Beverages—Soups

These are available in the following varieties—

(a) *Beverages*: Cocoa milk and malted milk;

(b) *Soups*: Kidney, mock turtle and oxtail.

At the request of operational troops these are available at 25 per cent beverages and 75 per cent soups.

The scale of issue is at the rate of 110 tins per 100 men per month.

Gross weight, one tin 20 oz.

Net weight, contents 13 oz. (2 full cups).

Hexamine Cookers

Hexamine cooker packs are available as—

(a) One pack containing one cooker with eight fuel tablets: weight 15 oz.

(b) One pack containing eight fuel tablets only: weight 15 oz.

Rum

Rum or tea may be issued in accordance with Allowance Regulations, paragraph 42, on the scale as laid down on page 5, Serial 31 of Ration Scales, East Africa, 1953.

Rum is issuable to European troops only. Tea will be issued to African troops.

CHAPTER XX

FIRST AID AND PREVENTIVE MEDICINE

Section 1—First Aid

1. It is essential that every man on operations should understand not only the basic methods of first aid to the injured, but also General Health, in other words the principles of Preventive Medicine. This, in particular, applies to senior and junior leaders who are responsible for the health of their men.

2. Many a soldier has been saved from death or permanent disability because immediate **first aid** was rendered, and many have died as the result of their comrades lacking the knowledge or the confidence to apply **first aid**.

3. **First Aid.**—First aid saves lives and stops pain; it is only common sense plus a little specialized knowledge.

   (a) **A lightly wounded man**, if given first aid, can go on fighting. It is therefore essential to act quickly.

   (b) **A badly wounded man** looks pale and sweaty. Be prepared for this. Calm him and also the men under your command.

   (c) **Don't disturb a wounded man** too much unless you have to. Nature will tell him how to lie in the safest and most comfortable position.

   (d) **Look, think and then act.** There may be three men wounded at once. Treat the most urgent first. Keep under cover. Any fool can be brave and get killed; be brave and don't get killed, and save your friend instead. Look, think and then act.

   (e) **Equipment:**—

   (i) First Field Dressing is carried by every man.

   (ii) Each section must carry a J. Pack.

   (iii) Extra medical equipment and dressings are carried by the medical orderlies.

   (iv) Stretchers (local pattern) are available, which consist of canvas only, without poles. The canvas can be carried folded in the pack, and poles provided when required by cutting bamboos, or any other suitable timber on the spot.

4. When a man gets hit beside you—
    Calm yourself.
    Stop his bleeding.
    Keep him warm.
    That is all you need to know.

5. **Wounds.**—At the time of injury pain is seldom felt. The sensation is very like a blow that you may get when boxing.

6. **When to Give a Man a Drink.**—Give any wounded man a drink of anything you have—but **do not** give a drink to a man with a wound in the belly, or to a man who cannot swallow. You will kill him if you do. Remember—no drink to these two men. But you can moisten their lips.

7. **Stop Bleeding.**—Bleeding of a slight or severe degree accompanies all wounds. A man can bleed to death very quickly. So **act promptly.** Remember bleeding can be stopped by the firm pressure of a dressing accurately applied on or into a wound. The dressing acts as a splint and helps to immobilize the injured part. After the dressing has been applied have faith and do not remove it to see if the bleeding has stopped.

8. **Shock.**—Shock lowers vitality; it kills more men than bullets. It is increased by fear, cold and pain. Restore by encouragement the peace of mind of the wounded man. Reassure him by the quiet methodical way you go about giving **first aid.** All movement of the wounded must be gentle and reduced to a minimum. Pain is allayed by immobilization. If pain is severe morphia should be given. If possible give hot sweet drinks—tea or soups.

9. **Abdominal Wounds.**—All cases should be treated as of first urgency. The object is to get the wounded man quickly and comfortably to surgical aid. **Don't give this man anything to drink.**

10. **Chest Wounds.**—The small perforating wound requires little direct attention save the application of a dressing. If the wounded man coughs up blood explain to him that it must be expected. Reassurance and calmness are essential for his peace of mind. The larger wounds are of the valve type and suck in air, they require immediate **first aid.** The man finds it

difficult to breathe. Seal the wounds off with elastoplast or the firm application of a dressing into the wound itself. Bind the dressing firmly to the chest. Transport the patient in the position most comfortable to himself.

11. **The Jaws and Face.**—The impact of the blow may cause a temporary loss of vision. The first sign is usually a trickle of blood on the face or in the mouth. The patient may faint. A patient with a severe jaw wound should be laid stomach down on the stretcher with his head projecting beyond the canvas and the forehead supported by a bandage sling between the handlebars. This prevent the man swallowing blood and saliva and his tongue falling back. Keep the foot of the stretcher higher than the head to ensure drainage.

12. **Broken Bones.**—To allay pain and shock and to prevent the splintered bones damaging blood vessels, nerves and muscles, the bones together with their surrounding tissues and muscles must be immobilized by splinting. Support the broken limb with a well padded splint. Place the limb in its most natural position and you can't go wrong. Don't let the limb flap around or the sharp ends of the splintered bones will cut the vessels, nerves and muscles to pieces. A broken arm should be bound firmly but not too tightly to the chest. After splinting the broken lower limb bind it to the other, foot to foot, knee to knee and thigh to thigh.

13. **Injury to Spine.**— In fractures and dislocations the affected part of the spine should be kept braced well back by ensuring that the stomach and chest are stuck out. The injured man with these reservations can be transported either lying on his back or abdomen.

14. (*a*) **Burns and Scalds.**—If a limb has been hurt elevate and immobilize it. The exposure method is the best form of treatment in this country. The affected part may be dusted with Penicillin powder. Allay pain if necessary by frequent drinks to which salt has been added.

(*b*) **Phosphorus Burns.**—Hold under water—pick out the pieces of phosphorus. Keep the wound wet.

15. **Artificial Respiration.**—For the apparently electrocuted of drowned. In the former case first free the victim from the

current without electrocuting yourself and then ensure that after this he is earthed. In the case of the apparently drowned after removing the man from the water he should be laid down with the head lower than the feet.

Back pressure—arm lift method of Holger Nielsen. (See diagram.)

(a) (i) Begin at once. Every second counts.

  Lay the casualty face downwards with head turned to one side, arms bent and forehead resting on his hands, so as to keep mouth and nose free from obstruction.

 (ii) Give one or two firm thumps with the flat of the hand between the shoulders to bring the tongue forward and clear the throat.

 (iii) Kneel at his head, placing one knee near the head and the other foot alongside the elbow. The operator's mid-line should be in line with that of the casualty. From time to time this position can be altered by changing the kneeling knee.

 (iv) Place your hands on his shoulder blades with thumbs touching on the mid-line and fingers towards the casualty's feet, your arms being kept straight and the heels of your hands over the spines of the shoulder blades.

(b) Bend forward with arms straight and apply light pressure by the weight of the upper part of your body while steadily counting "One, two and three". Time, 2¼ seconds. This forces the air out of the lungs.

(c) (i) Release the pressure gradually and slide your hands to just above the elbows of the casualty, counting "Four". Time, 1 second.

 (ii) Draw his arms and shoulders towards you by bending backwards with your arms straight till you feel resistance and tension, without lifting the chest off the ground, counting "Five, six and seven". Time, 2¼ seconds. This draws air into the lungs.

(d) Lay his arms and replace your hands on the shoulder blades counting "Eight". Time, 1 second.

(e) Repeat the movements with rhythmic rocking at the rate of approximately nine times to the minute, counting as follows:—

"One, two and three": with hands on shoulder blades, bend forwards and apply pressure (2¼ seconds).

"Four": slide hands to elbows (1 second).

"Five, six and seven": bend backwards raising arms and shoulders (2¼ seconds).

"Eight": lay arms down and place your hands on shoulder blades (1 second).

(f) When breathing is re-established omit the back pressure and continue the arm raising and lowering alone at the rate of 12 times to the minute, counting as follows:—

"One, two and three": arm raising (inspiration, 2¼ seconds).

"Four, five and six": arm lowering (expiration, 2¼ seconds).

DIAGRAM—ARTIFICIAL RESPIRATION

The Correct Starting Position.—(*Note the position of the rescuer's knee, foot and hands*)

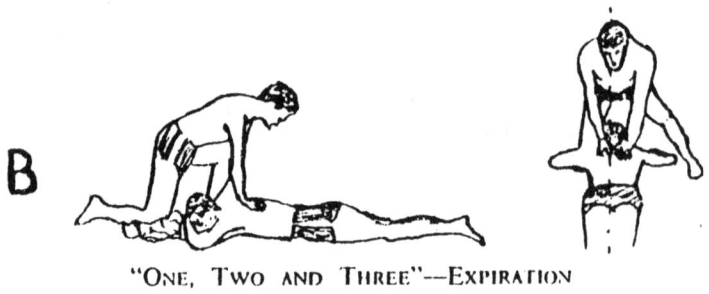

"One, Two and Three"—Expiration

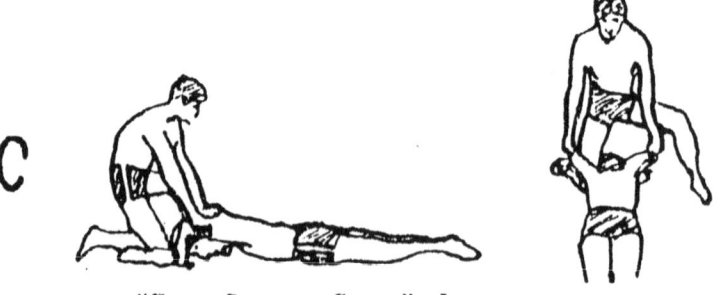

"Five, Six and Seven"—Inspiration

16. Snake Bite.—Rarely occurs in East Africa.
(a) Look at the bite:—
    (i) Multiple small punctures are non-poisonous.
    (ii) Two fang marks are due to a poisonous snake.
(b) Treatment:—
    (i) Apply a tourniquet to stop the flow of the blood in the vein.
    (ii) Incise the punctures and swollen areas to a depth of one-quarter inch to get free bleeding.
    (iii) Suck out the venom. Spit it out.
    (iv) Apply a dressing.

Section 2—First Aid to Health

Acclimatization

17. Much of the operational area of **Kenya** is composed of mountainous country, and troops are required to carry out tasks at heights of 8,000 to 13,000 feet, or even higher. Before men can do this with full physical efficiency, they require a period to become acclimatized. A month is usually allotted for the process. During that time, men are given increasingly strenuous exercise, until at the end of the month they are fully accustomed to live, work and fight, at high altitudes.

18. Unacclimatized men run a definite risk at such heights. Cases of heart failure, and of pneumonia, have occurred. If pneumonia develops, the patient should be sent down as quickly as possible to warmer, moister climates. Oral penicillin should be carried with the patrol, or dropped, if necessary, for the treatment of such cases.

19. Heavy breathing in thin air causes drying of the respiratory tracts. Men should therefore take particular care to drink plenty of fluids.

Malaria

20. Malaria is prevalent throughout **Kenya**, except in certain parts of the Highlands, and in the higher mountain ranges. It occurs in pockets throughout the Kikuyu reserve, but its distribution is not accurately mapped. For this reason, and because of frequent moves of troops, paludrine (for British troops) and mepacrine (for African troops) must be taken by all, wherever stationed in Kenya.

21. **Paludrine.**—One tablet daily while exposed to risk of infection beginning one day before being exposed. If unable to begin the day before being exposed to infection, three tablets to be taken on the first day and thereafter one tablet daily. One tablet daily for seven days after ceasing to be exposed, e.g. on return to U.K.

22. **Mepacrine.**—Two tablets daily for seven days before being exposed to risk of infection. One tablet daily while exposed. One tablet daily for 28 days after ceasing to be exposed.

23. There should be a strict unit routine for administration of paludrine and mepacrine; given at a fixed time, preferably on parade, and a register kept.

24. Troops proceeding on leave will be issued with sufficient paludrine (or mepacrine for A.O.R.) to cover the period of leave, and instructed to take one tablet daily. British troops proceeding to the U.K. must be issued with sufficient paludrine to take one tablet daily for seven days after leaving East Africa.

25. In some areas it is necessary to use mosquito nets, when this is advised by the medical officer. Apart from the risk of malaria, units may use nets as protection against nuisance mosquitoes and other insects.

26. Mosquito repellent is available for the use of men on night patrols, and should be issued by units if there appears to be a need for it.

Dysentery and Fly-borne Diseases

27. Every effort must be made to ensure that food is kept clean during carriage and preparation. Water must be purified before being drunk. Good camp sanitation MUST be maintained. Latrines must be kept clean, and closing of lids enforced. Grease traps must be cleaned daily. Refuse, including tins, must be burned, and subsequently buried. D.D.T. residual spray must be used in camps. Knapsack

sprayers are issued on a scale of one per company. Anti-fly spray and flit guns must be drawn up and used.

Schistomiasis

28. This disease is widely distributed in East Africa. Infection occurs by drinking, or bathing, in infected waters. Strict attention will be given to purification of water (*see* paragraph 29 below). Bathing in natural waters is prohibited, except in fast-flowing, rocky streams above 6,500 feet.

29. **Water.**—Drinking water must be purified by boiling, or by one of the recognized methods of chlorination before consumption. For individual use on patrols, Millbank Bags and individual water sterilizing outfits are available. Men who drink water straight from streams in an inhabited area lay themselves open to grave risk of disease.

Midget water filters, and portable water filters are also available.

The individual outfit is used as follows:—

(*a*) The water bottle is filled with water, as clean as is obtainable.

(*b*) A white tablet from the individual outfit is added and the bottle shaken.

(*c*) After half an hour the water is fit to drink.

(*d*) A blue tablet added at this time (*not before*) will remove the taste of chlorine.

(*e*) Cloudy water cannot be properly sterilized by chlorination. It can be strained through a Millbank Bag (issued to all units). Purification should then be carried out as detailed above. Boiling (or, if desired, making tea) will purify any water.

Skin Diseases

30. Newly arrived troops are very liable to skin damage by sunburn. The skin must be gradually exposed, until well tanned. Arms and knees are particularly liable to damage.

31. Good ablution arrangements are essential, improvising where necessary, since skin cleanliness is the prime prevention of skin disease.

32. Care of the feet is of prime importance. Feet must be kept clean, socks regularly washed, changed and darned. Foot powder is available, and should be used.

Venereal Diseases

33. Venereal Diseases are prevalent. Troops must be warned against venereal diseases, especially when going on leave. They must be told of the existence of Prophylactic Centres, and instructed to use them if exposed to infection. Sheaths and prophylactic packets are available from these centres. Regular F.F.I. inspections must be held.

Section 3—Evacuation of Casualties

General

34. Every unit has its own Medical Officers, its own small medical staff and its own Medical Reception Station (M.R.S.). This M.R.S. is either tented or hutted, comprises 4-6 beds and is run entirely by the unit. The policy is to hold a patient for a day to avoid the evacuation of mild cases who can then be returned direct to duty.

35. Evacuation of sick or wounded is normally carried out by ambulance car. Every unit has its own ambulance car and the R.M.O.s have Land Rovers which are readily convertible to take a stretcher.

36. Evacuation is usually to the Military Hospitals at Nanyuki, Nyeri or Nairobi. There is, however, alternative medical cover in Embu, Meru and Fort Hall, where there are African Civil Hospitals run by European staff. Throughout the Emergency these hospitals have been most helpful and co-operative and are always prepared to accept any of our patients when considered necessary. Our R.M.O.s and the civil M.O.s are in close touch.

Air Evacuation

37. There are a number of air strips now in use for small aircraft and the building of others is undertaken as required for major operations. From an evacuation point of view these strips are invaluable. In order to accelerate evacuation the R.M.O., through the unit, contacts Medical Branch at General Headquarters. Med then contact the Kenya Police Reserve Air Wing and a plane, suitably equipped with stretcher, is despatched and evacuates the casualty to the nearest hospital.

GENERAL HEADQUARTERS,
EAST AFRICA,
NAIROBI.
27th November, 1954.

www.ingramcontent.com/pod-product-compliance
Lightning Source LLC
Chambersburg PA
CBHW061604110426
42742CB00039B/2771